MEND
A STORY OF DIVORCE

Written by **SOPHIA RECCA**

Art by **NAM KIM** and **GARRY LEACH**

Colors by **FAHRIZA KAMAPUTRA**

Lettering by **JIMMY BETANCOURT**
for Comicraft

Zuiker Press

Los Angeles

MEND: A STORY OF DIVORCE

© 2018 Zuiker Press

Sophia Recca Photographs © 2018 Sophia Recca

Written by Anthony E. Zuiker
Art by Nam Kim and Garry Leach
Colors by Fahriza Kamaputra
Lettering by Jimmy Betancourt for Comicraft
Designed by Roberta Melzl
Edited by Dave Elliott

Founders: Michelle & Anthony E. Zuiker
Publisher: Sven Larsen

Published by Zuiker Press
16255 Ventura Blvd.,
Suite #900
Encino, CA 91436
United States of America

Publicity by Jonalyn Morris PR
jonalyn@jonalynmorrispr.com and info@zuikerpress.com

Visit us online at www.zuikerpress.com

Library of Congress Catalog-in-Publication data is
available upon request.
ISBN 978-1-947378-00-1 (hardcover)

PRINTED IN CANADA
November 2018
8 7 6 5 4 3 2 1

DEDICATED TO ... every young person who needs to be reminded they are not alone.

HOPE lies within these pages.

ZUIKER PRESS

... is a husband and wife publishing company that champions the voices of young authors. We are an **ISSUE-BASED** literary house. All of our authors have elected to tell their personal stories and be the ambassadors of their cause. Their goal, as is ours, is that young people will learn from the pain and heroics of our authors and find **HOPE**, **HAPPINESS** and **CHANGE** in their own lives.

TEACHER'S CORNER

SHANNON LIVELY

is an educator with a bachelor's degree in elementary education from the University of Nevada, Las Vegas, and a master's degree from Southern Utah University, as well as advanced degrees in differentiated instruction and technology. In 2013, she was awarded the Barrick Gold One Classroom at a Time grant, then chosen as Teacher of the Year. She is currently completing the National Board Certification while teaching fifth grade at John C. Vanderburg Elementary School in Henderson, Nevada.

WHY WE HONOR TEACHERS

We understand the hard work it takes to be a teacher! It takes a lot of time to prepare work for students. At Zuiker Press, we want to give teachers access to class work with each book we publish. We will have a **TEACHER'S CORNER** area on our website, Zuikerpress.com, which will give teachers class work beyond the story. This is where you can partake in discussions, comprehension, reading groups, and other activities with your students. All of these printable resources will be under the umbrella of Common Core to stay consistent with how subjects are being taught. We hope this helps teachers utilize each story to the fullest extent!

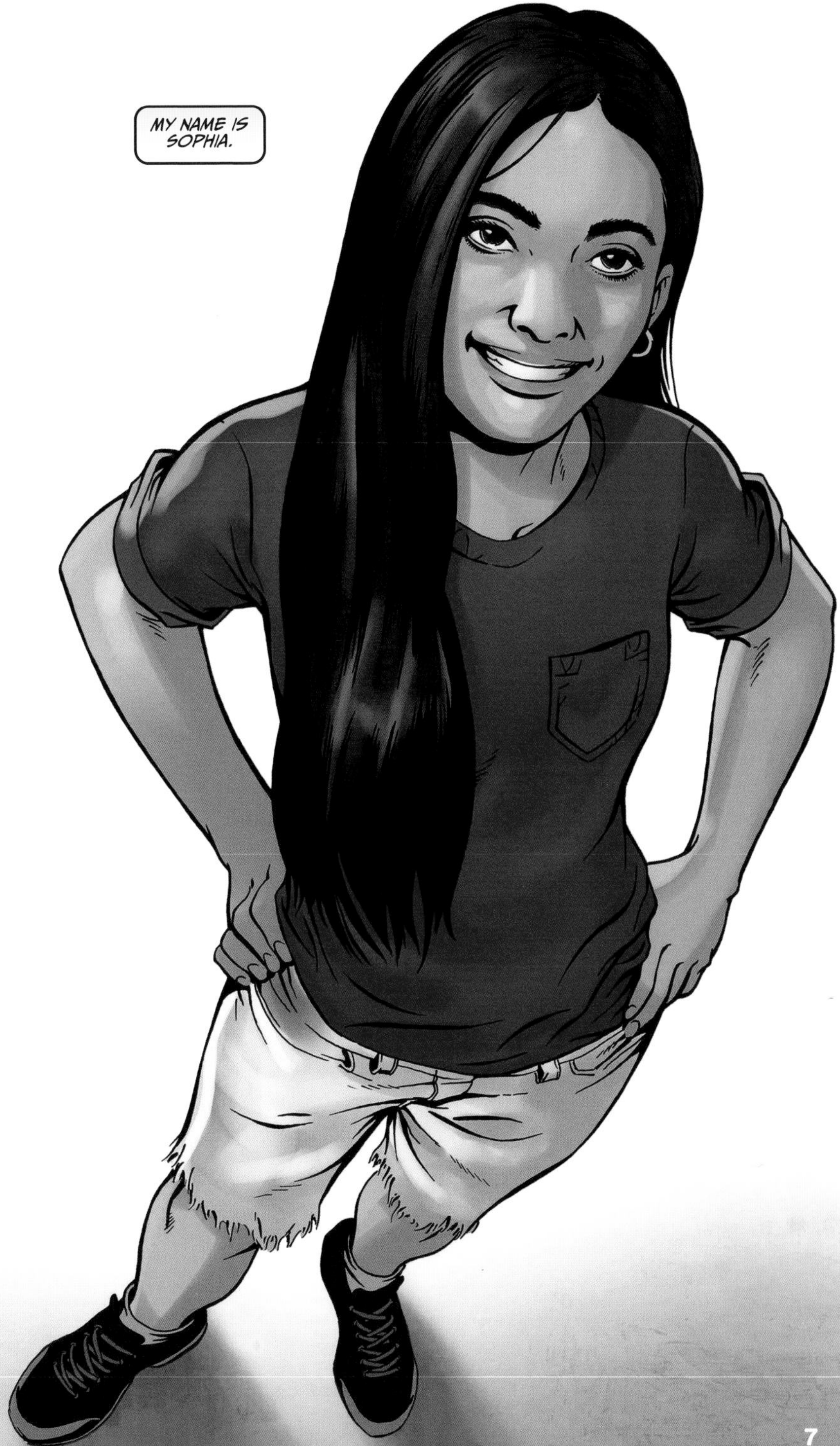
MY NAME IS SOPHIA.

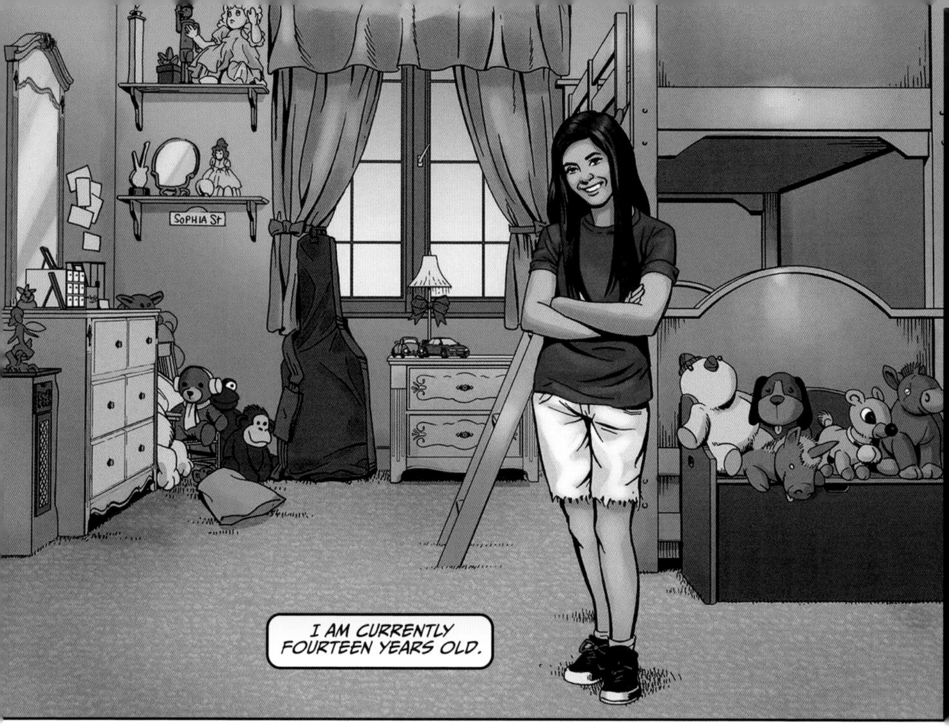
SOPHIA St
I AM CURRENTLY FOURTEEN YEARS OLD.

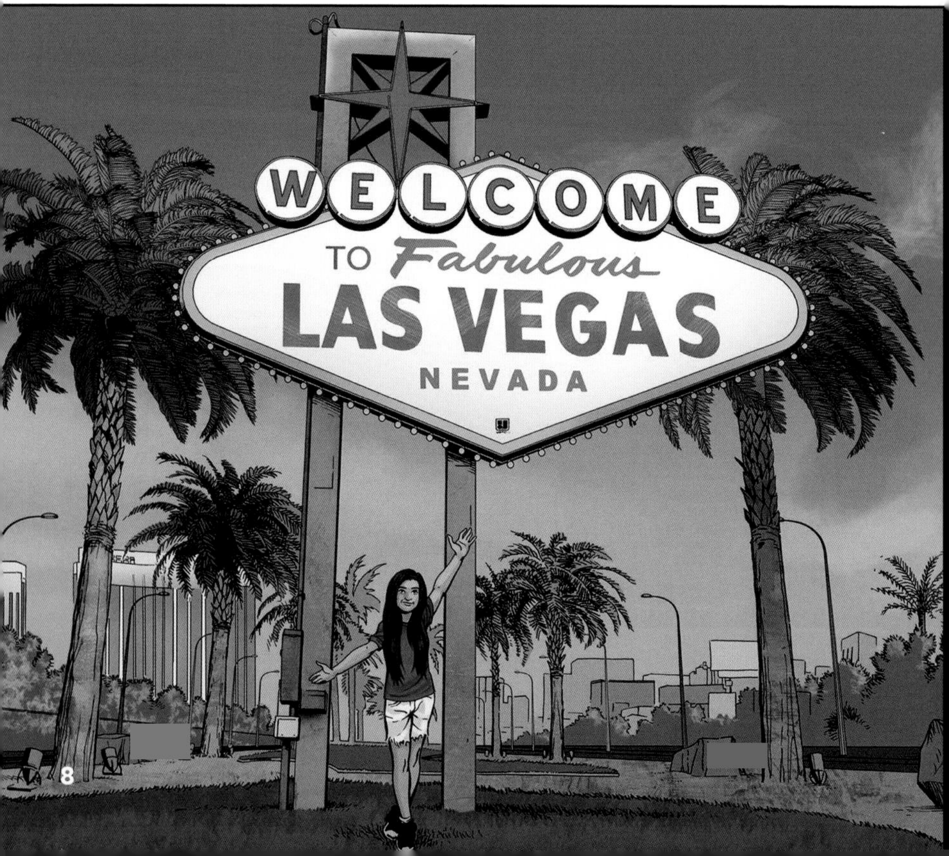
WELCOME
TO Fabulous
LAS VEGAS
NEVADA

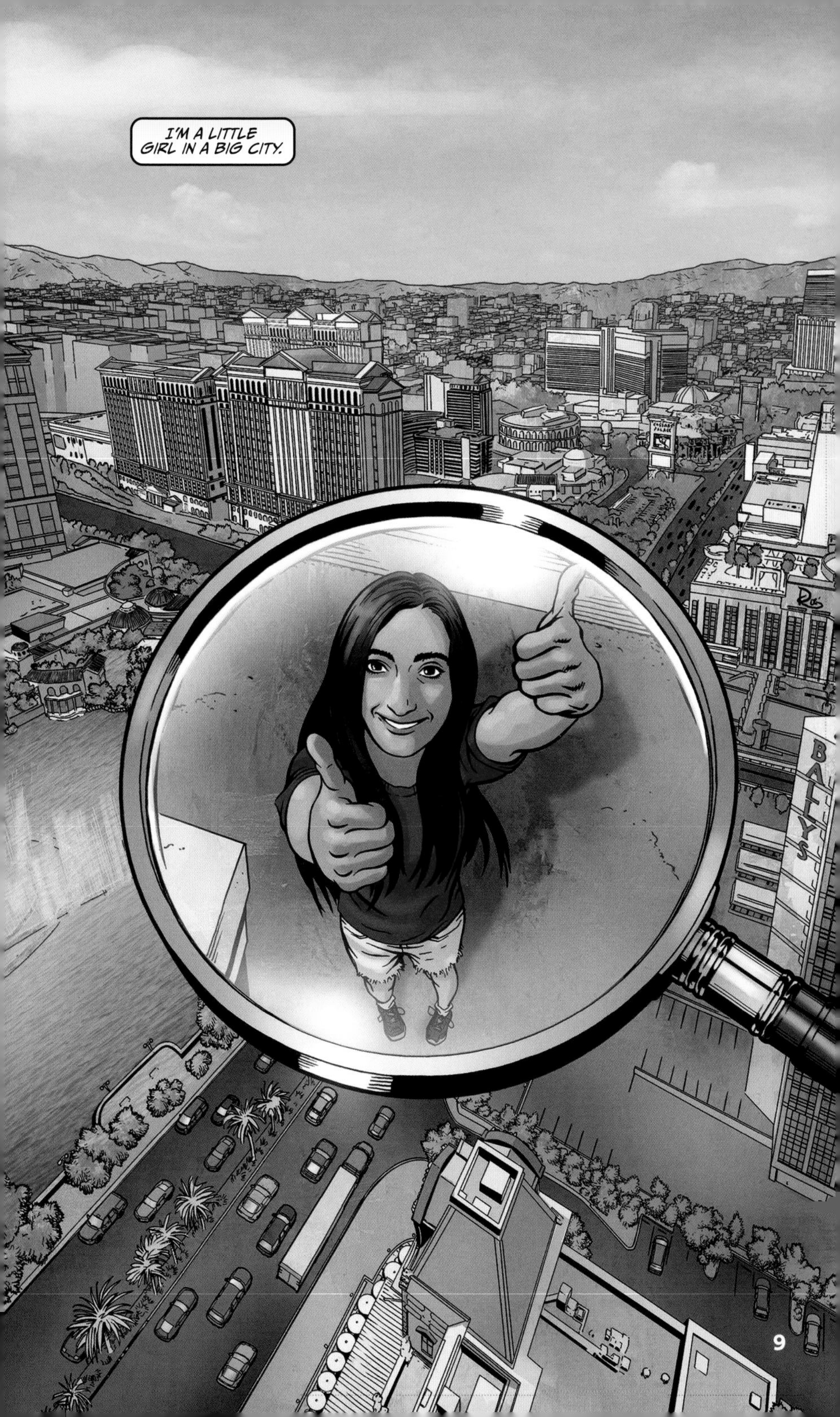
I'M A LITTLE GIRL IN A BIG CITY.
CAESARS PALACE
BALLY'S

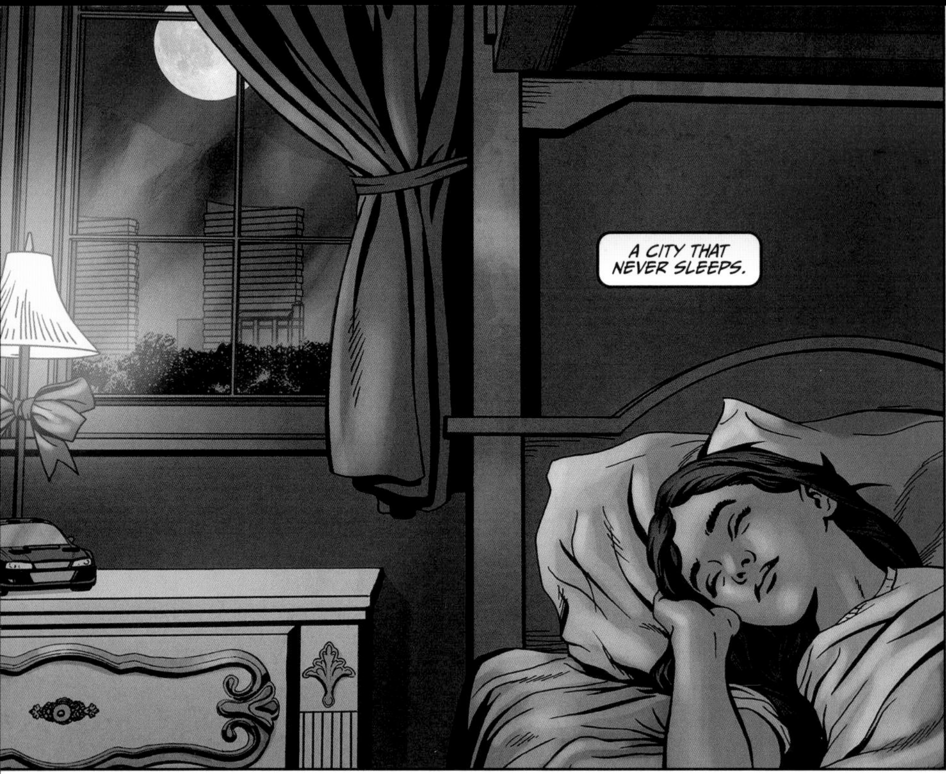
A CITY THAT NEVER SLEEPS.

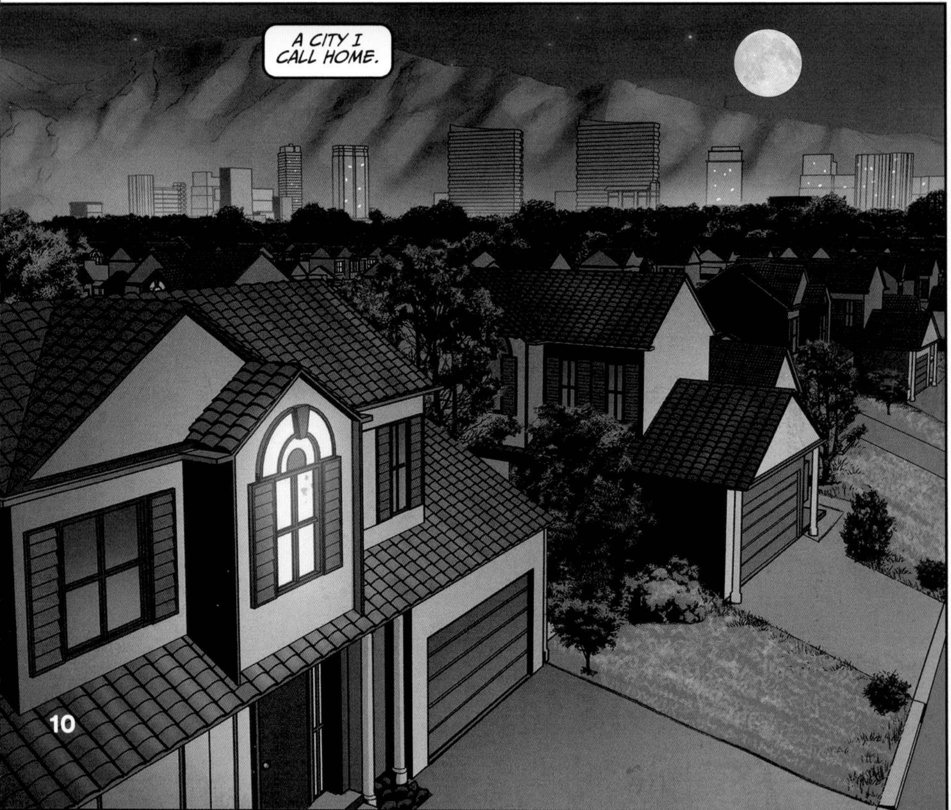
A CITY I CALL HOME.

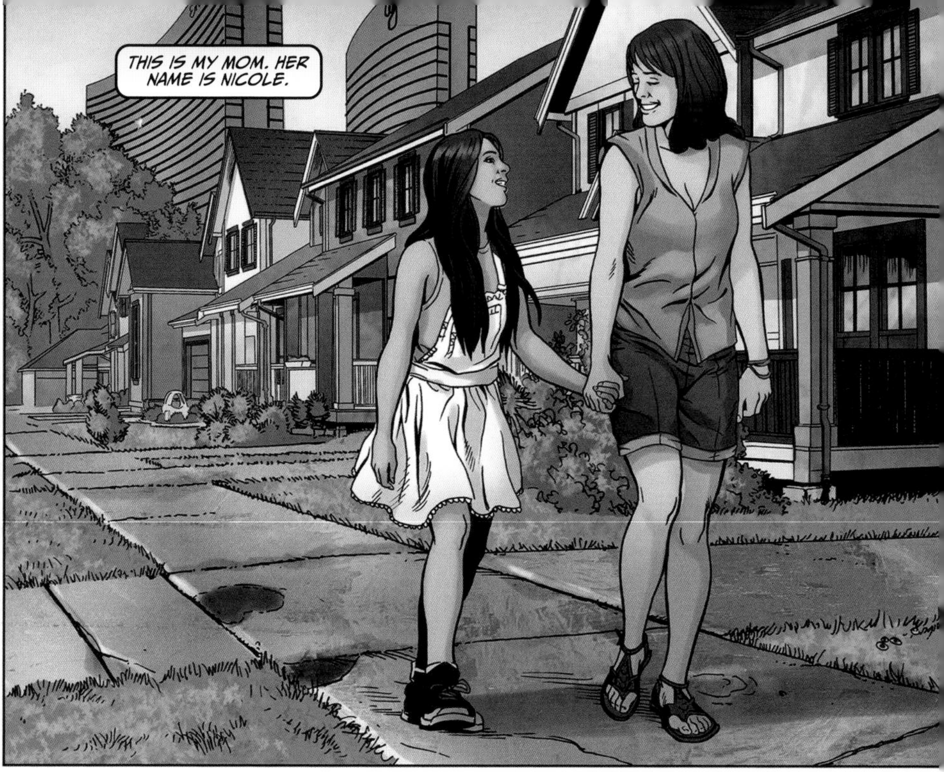
THIS IS MY MOM. HER NAME IS NICOLE.

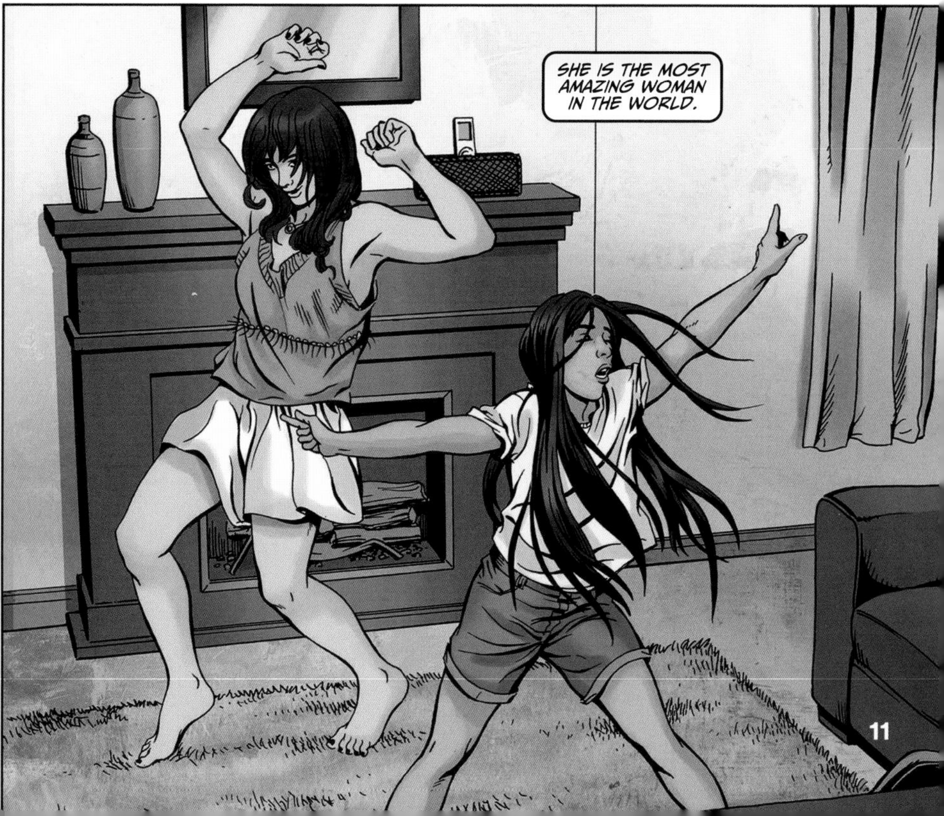
SHE IS THE MOST AMAZING WOMAN IN THE WORLD.

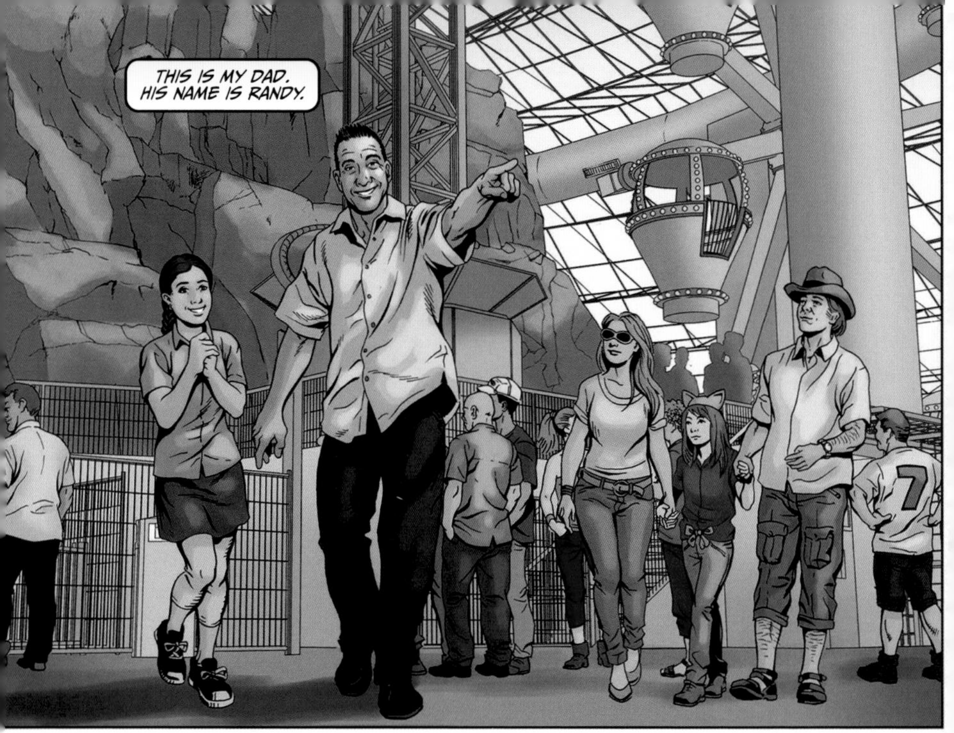
THIS IS MY DAD.
HIS NAME IS RANDY.

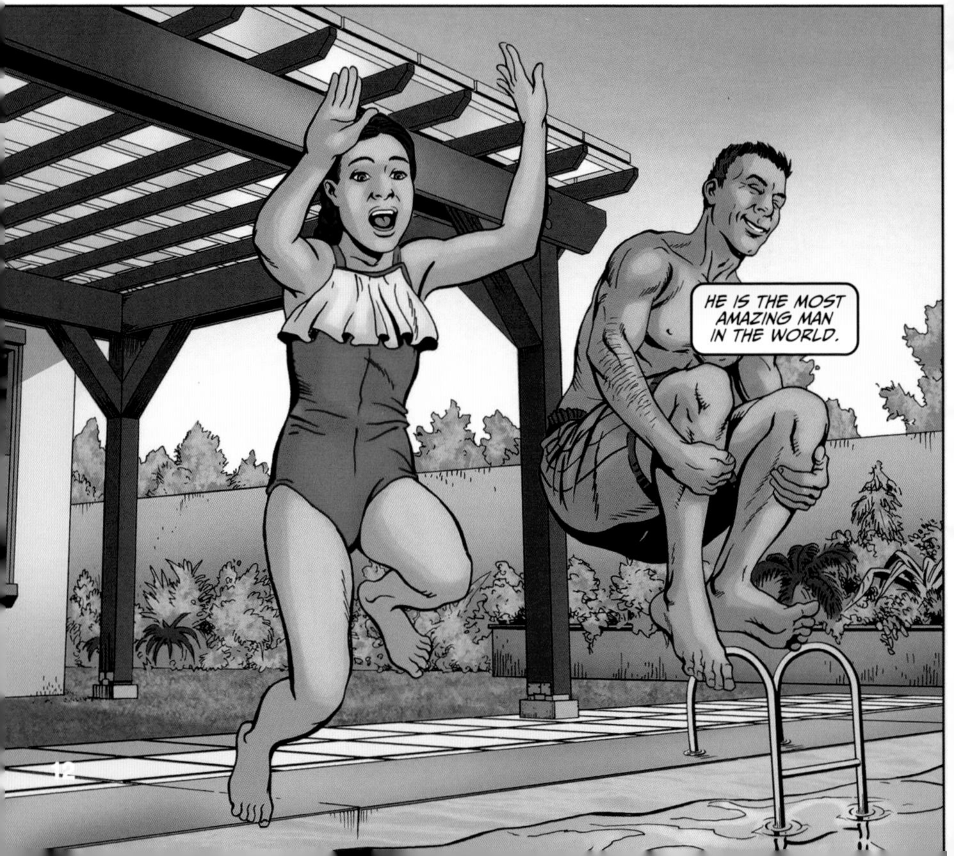
HE IS THE MOST
AMAZING MAN
IN THE WORLD.

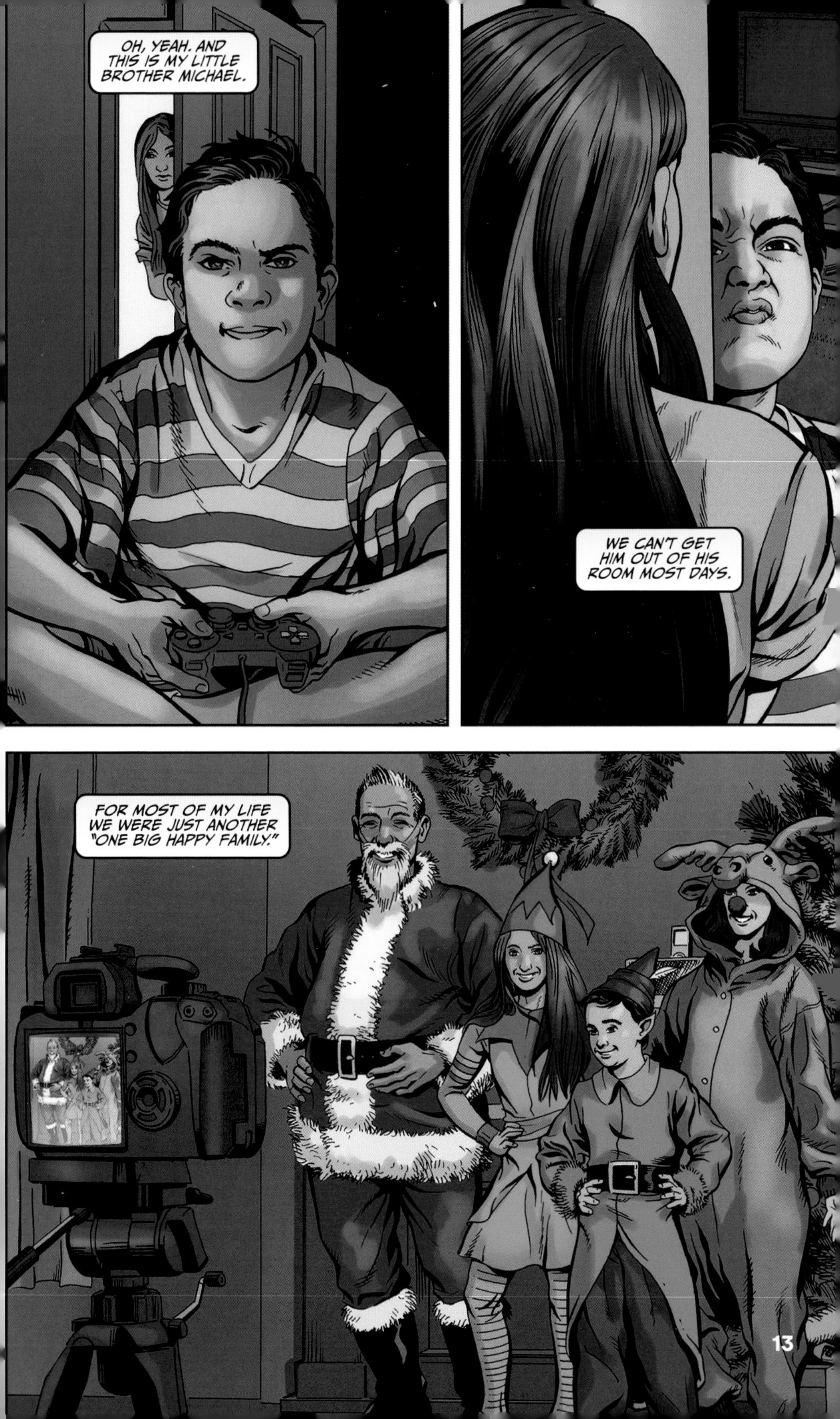
OH, YEAH. AND THIS IS MY LITTLE BROTHER MICHAEL.
WE CAN'T GET HIM OUT OF HIS ROOM MOST DAYS.
FOR MOST OF MY LIFE WE WERE JUST ANOTHER "ONE BIG HAPPY FAMILY."

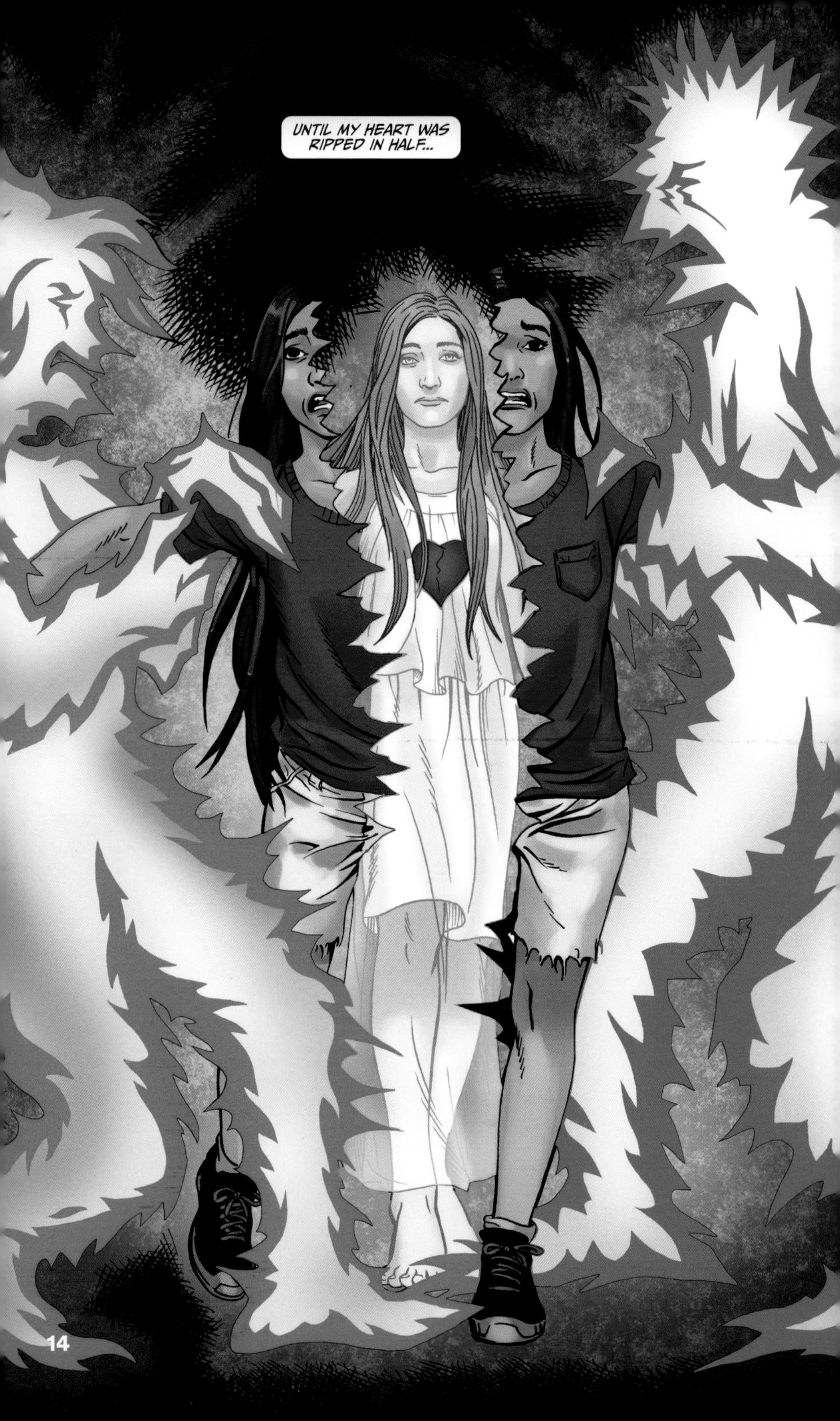
UNTIL MY HEART WAS RIPPED IN HALF...

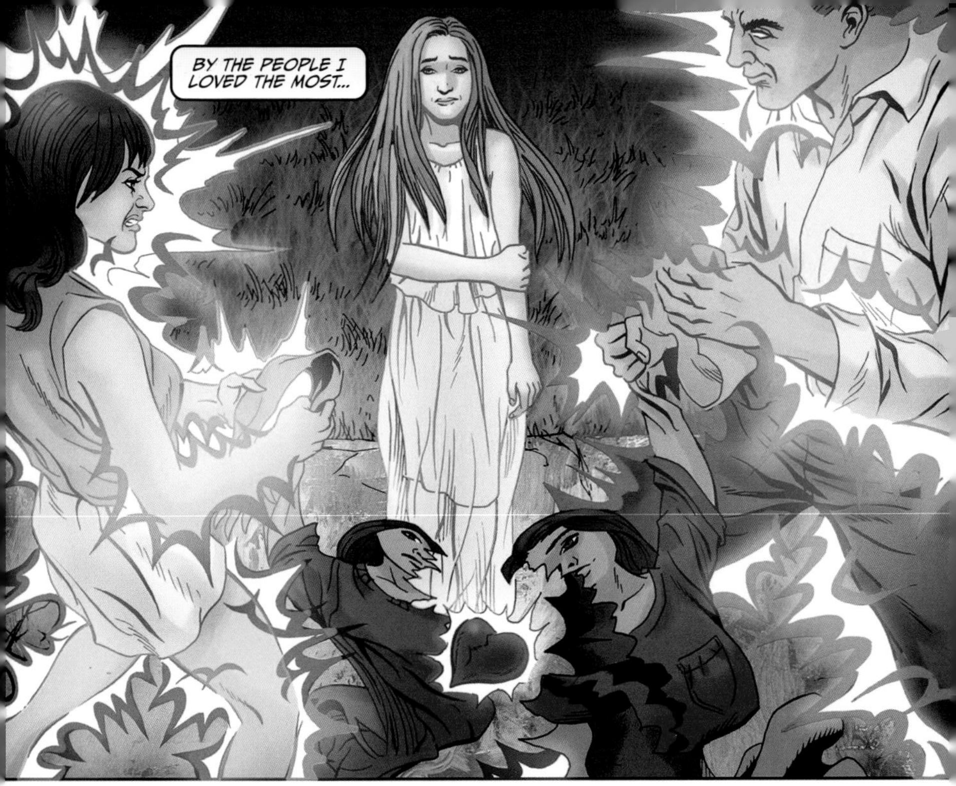
BY THE PEOPLE I
LOVED THE MOST...

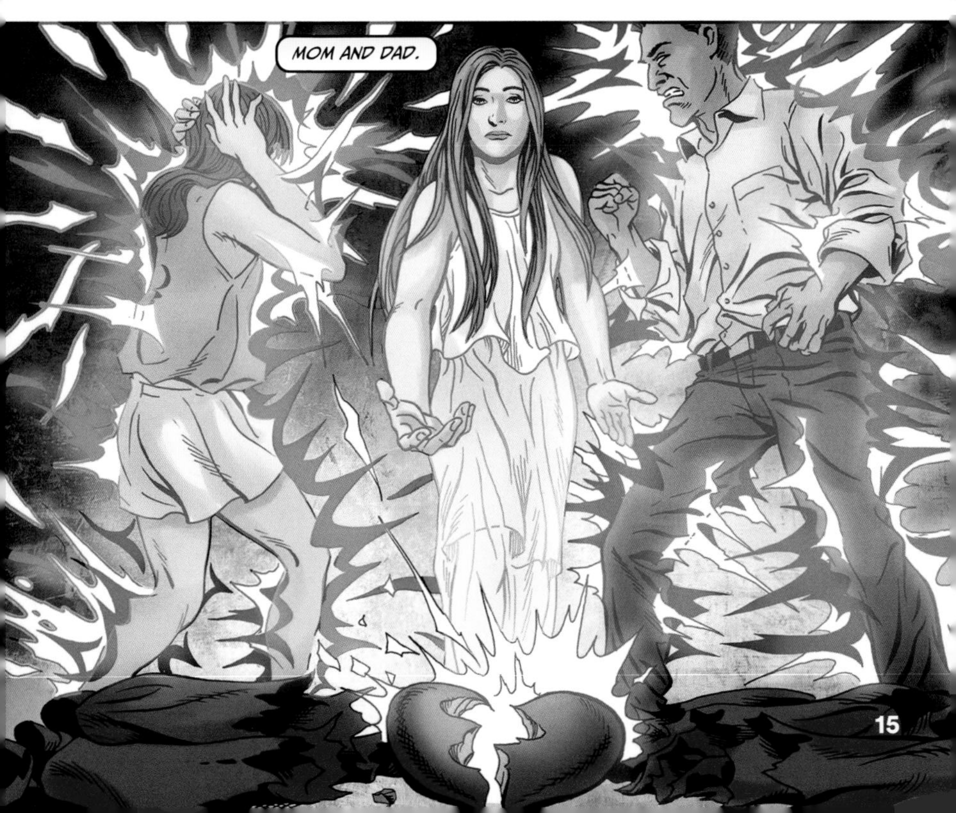
MOM AND DAD.

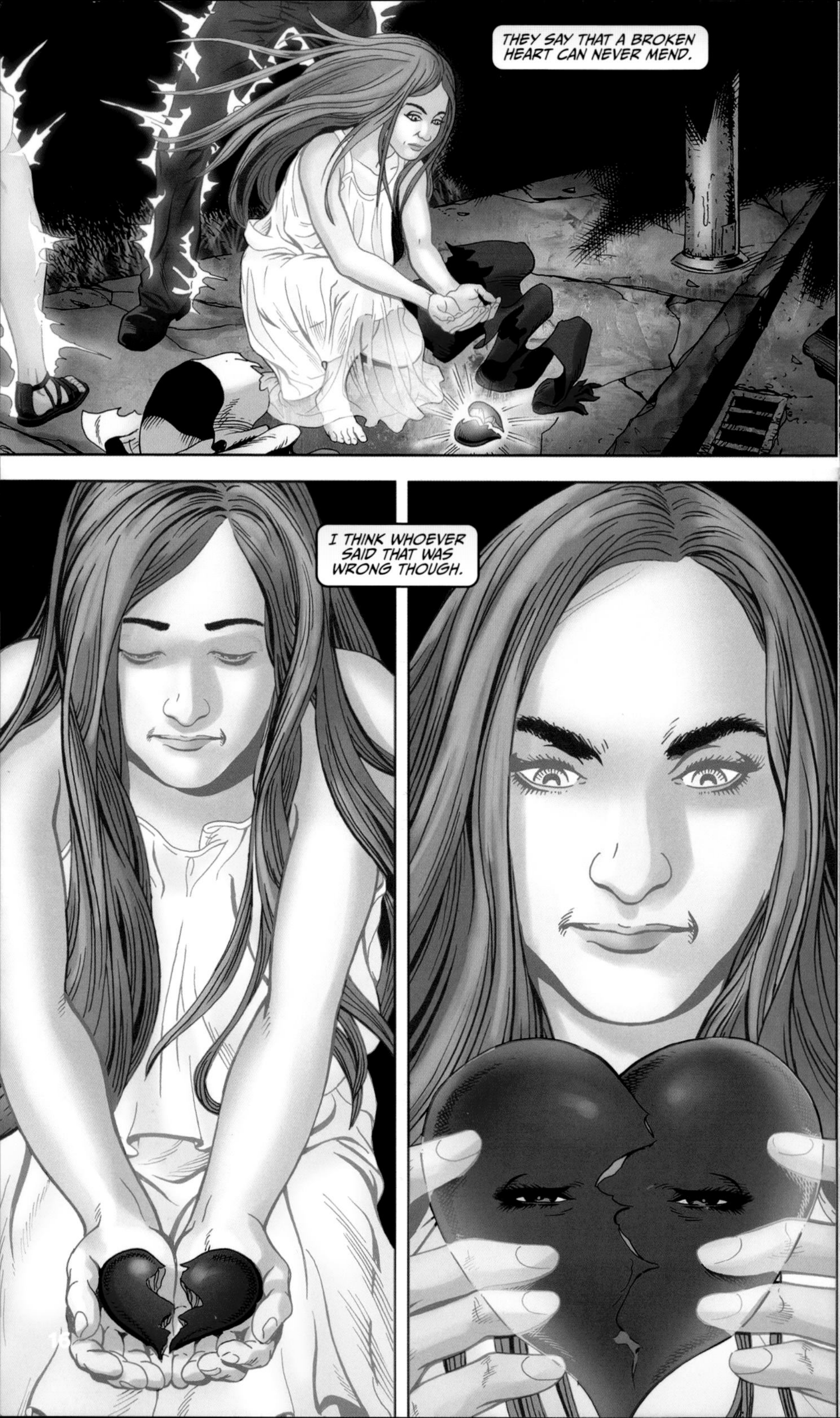
THEY SAY THAT A BROKEN HEART CAN NEVER MEND.
I THINK WHOEVER SAID THAT WAS WRONG THOUGH.

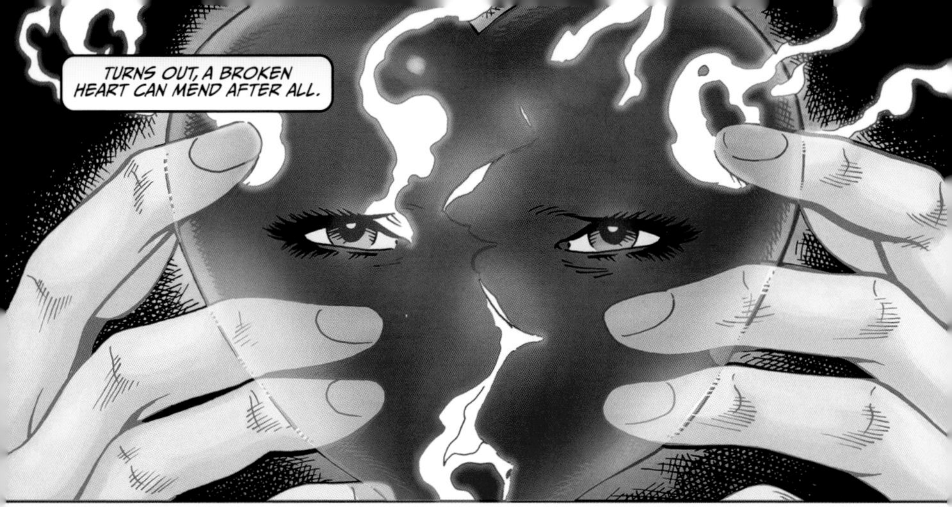
TURNS OUT, A BROKEN HEART CAN MEND AFTER ALL.

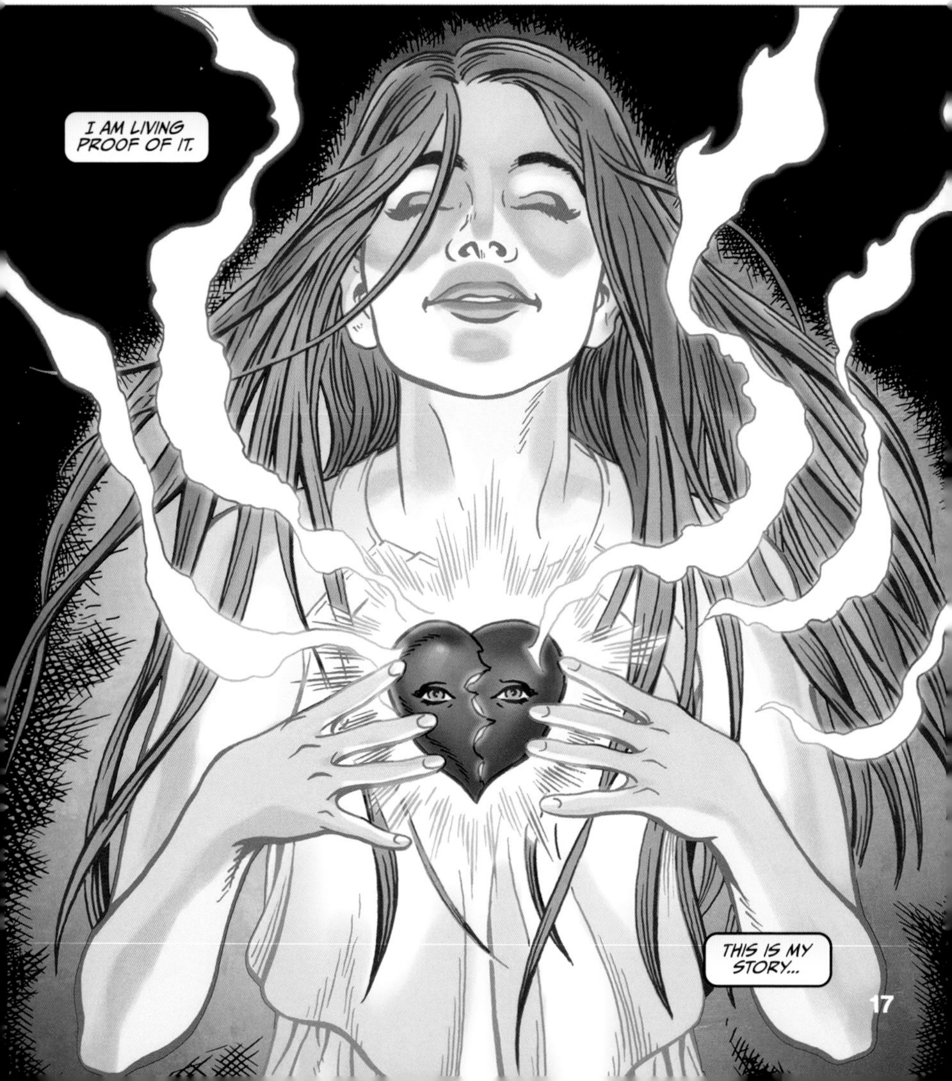
I AM LIVING PROOF OF IT.
THIS IS MY STORY...

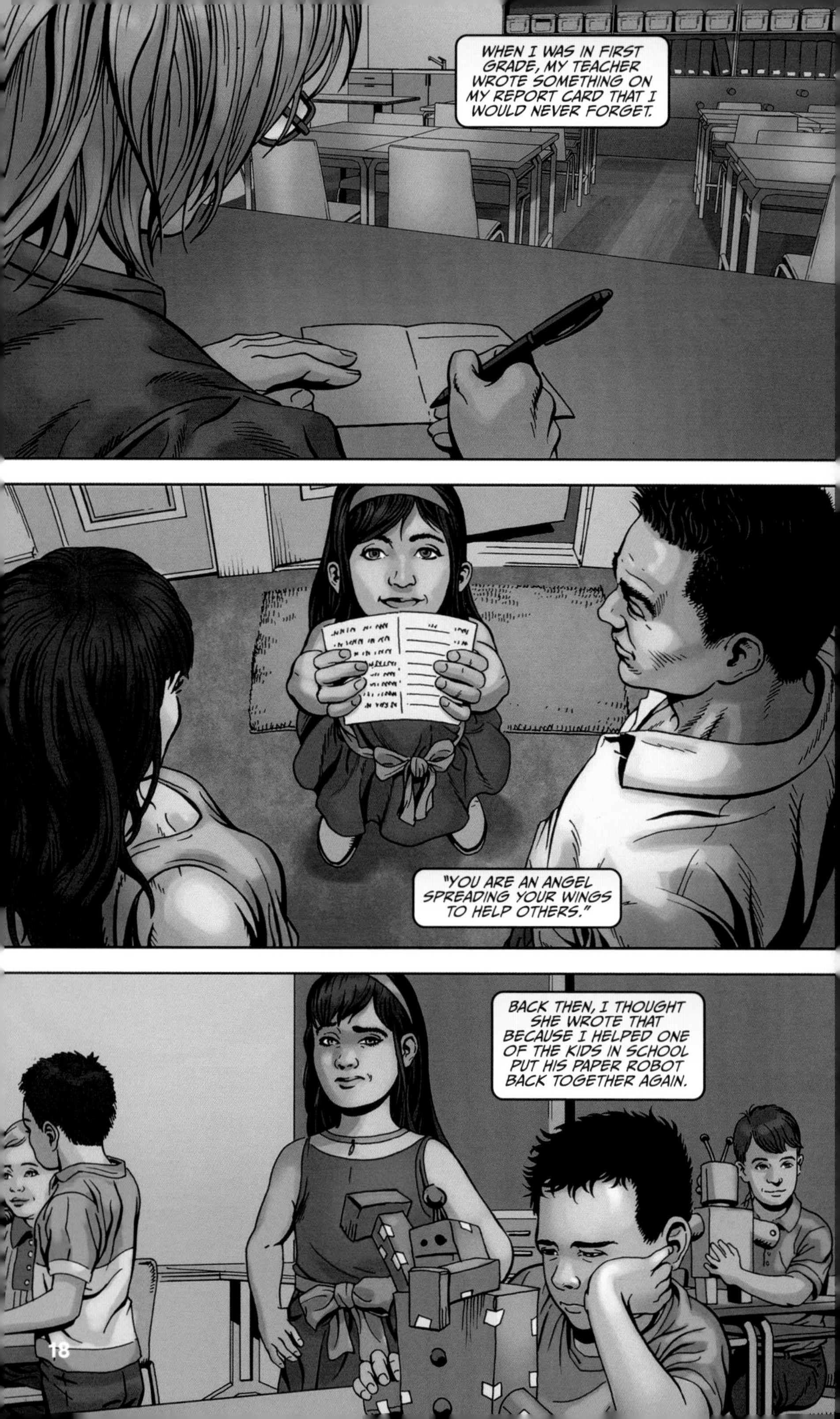

WHEN I WAS IN FIRST GRADE, MY TEACHER WROTE SOMETHING ON MY REPORT CARD THAT I WOULD NEVER FORGET.
"YOU ARE AN ANGEL SPREADING YOUR WINGS TO HELP OTHERS."
BACK THEN, I THOUGHT SHE WROTE THAT BECAUSE I HELPED ONE OF THE KIDS IN SCHOOL PUT HIS PAPER ROBOT BACK TOGETHER AGAIN.

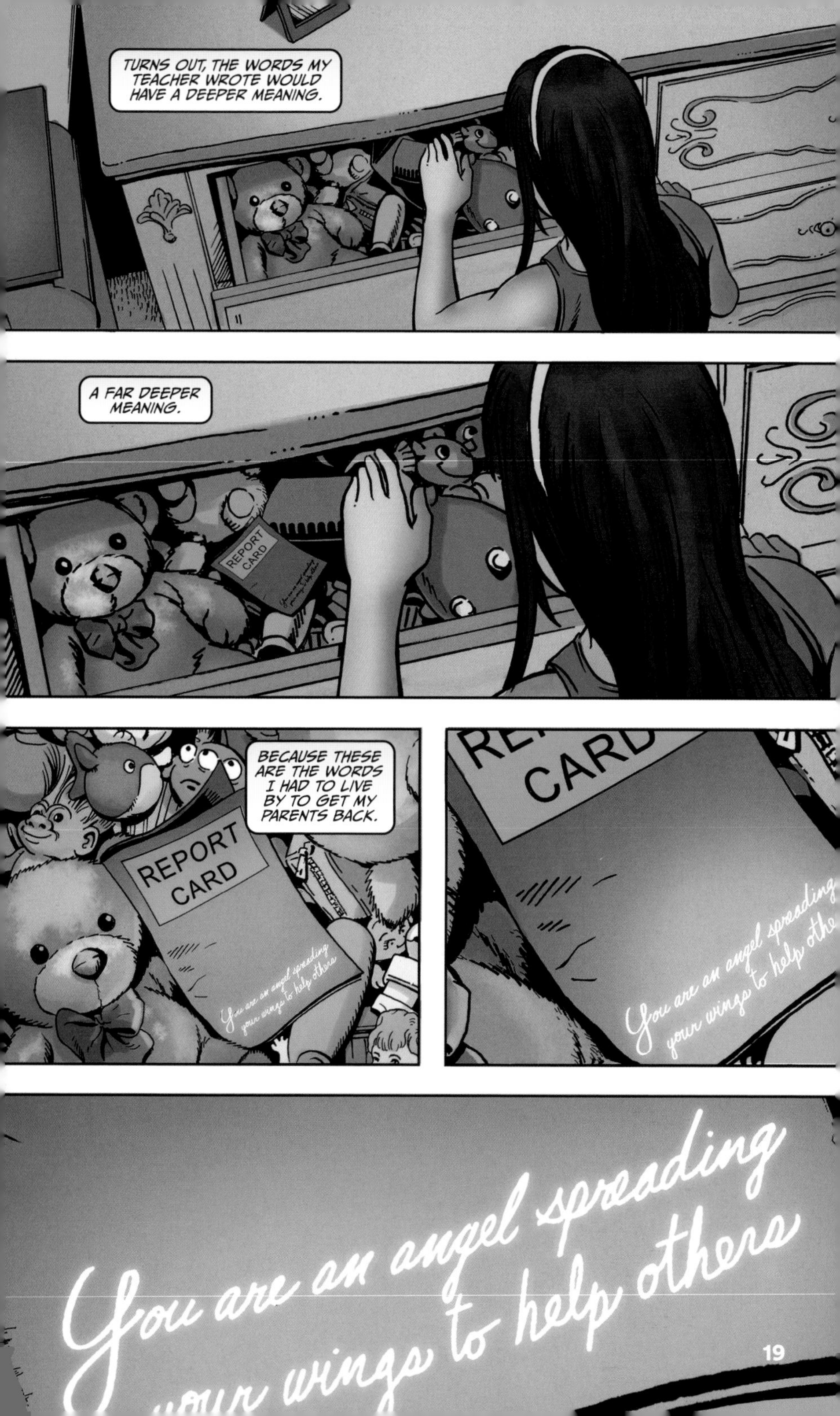
TURNS OUT, THE WORDS MY TEACHER WROTE WOULD HAVE A DEEPER MEANING.
A FAR DEEPER MEANING.
REPORT CARD
BECAUSE THESE ARE THE WORDS I HAD TO LIVE BY TO GET MY PARENTS BACK.
REPORT CARD
You are an angel spreading your wings to help others
CARD
You are an angel spreading your wings to help othe
You are an angel spreading your wings to help others

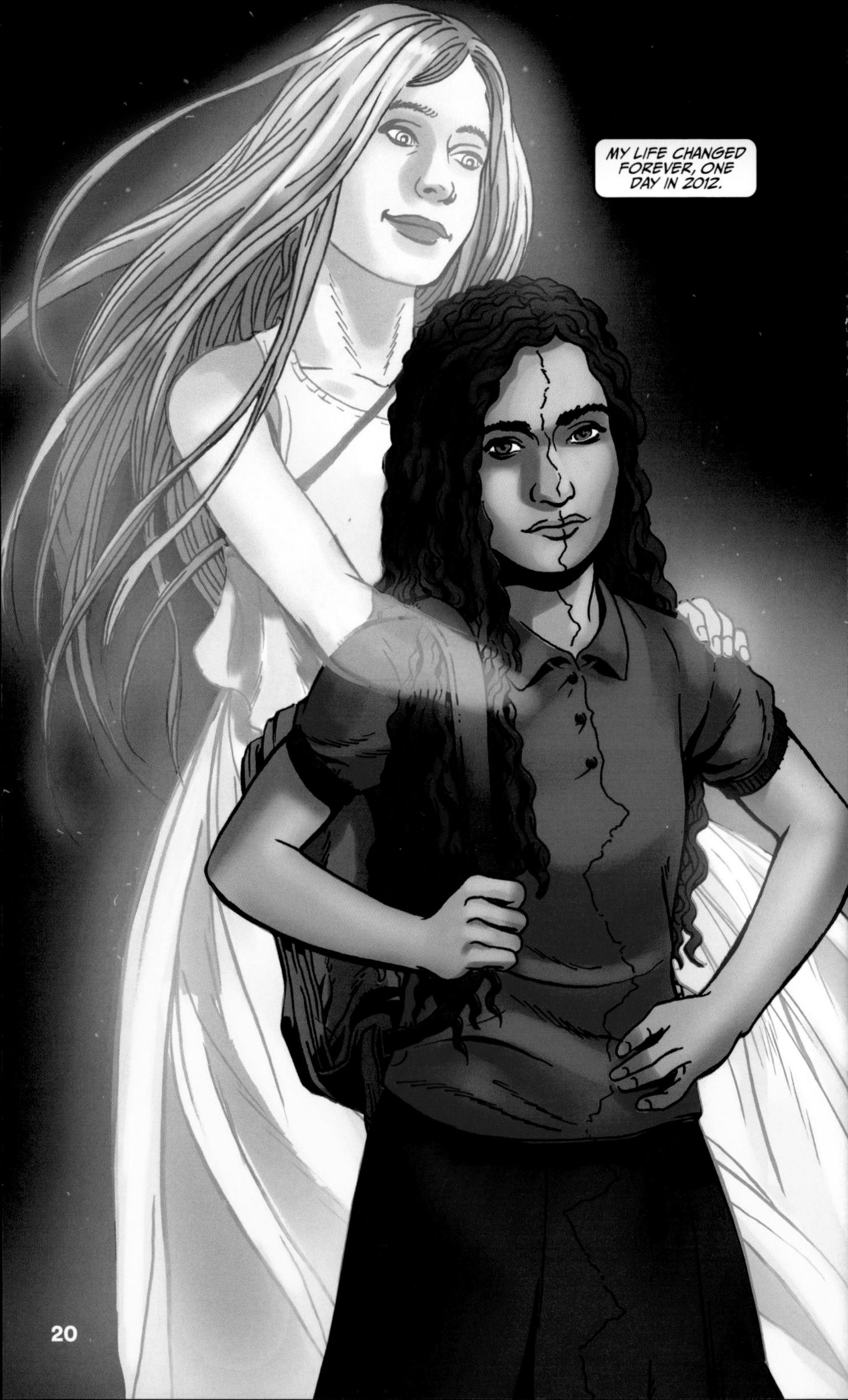
MY LIFE CHANGED FOREVER, ONE DAY IN 2012.

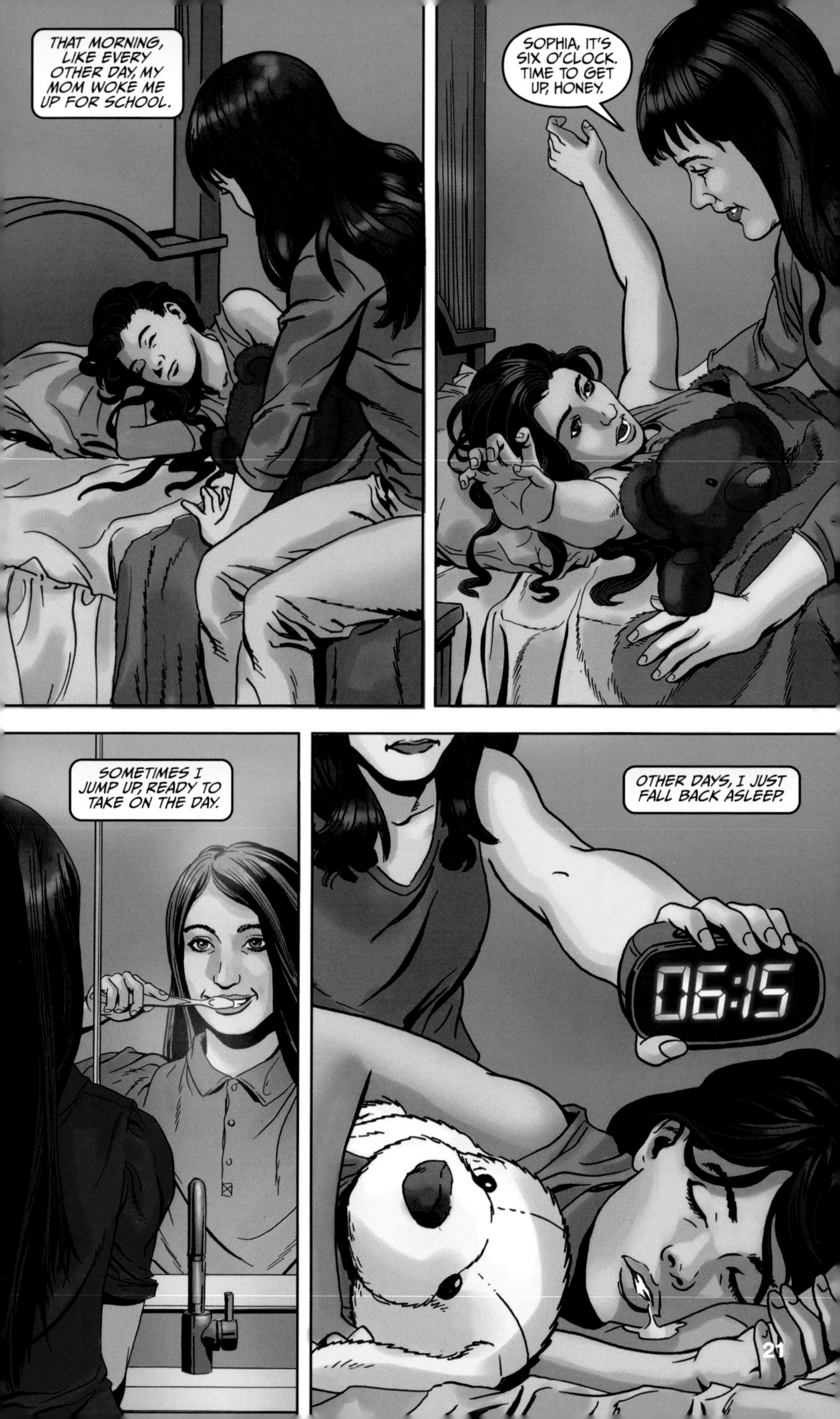
THAT MORNING, LIKE EVERY OTHER DAY, MY MOM WOKE ME UP FOR SCHOOL.
SOPHIA, IT'S SIX O'CLOCK. TIME TO GET UP, HONEY.
SOMETIMES I JUMP UP, READY TO TAKE ON THE DAY.
OTHER DAYS, I JUST FALL BACK ASLEEP.
06:15

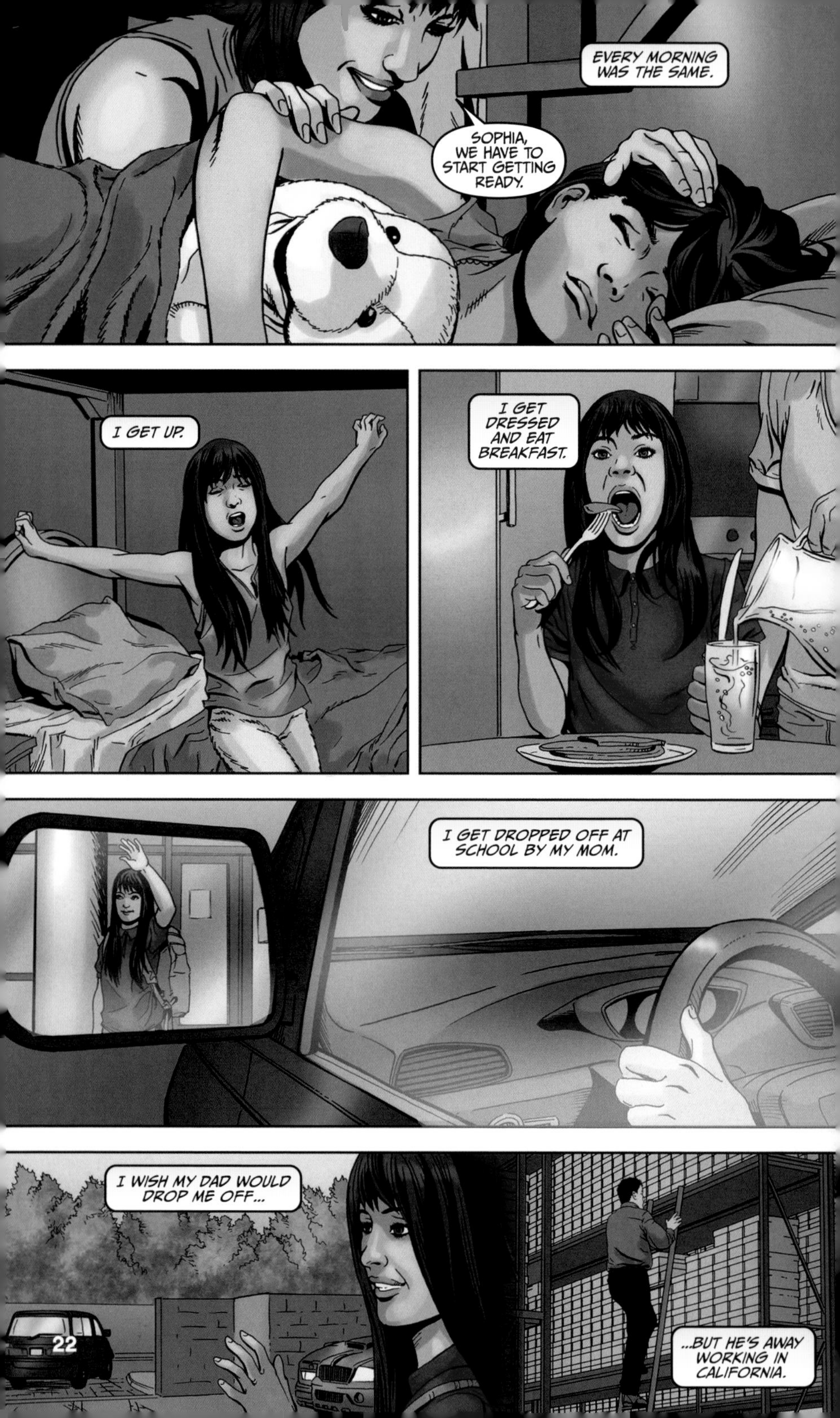
EVERY MORNING WAS THE SAME.
SOPHIA, WE HAVE TO START GETTING READY.
I GET UP.
I GET DRESSED AND EAT BREAKFAST.
I GET DROPPED OFF AT SCHOOL BY MY MOM.
I WISH MY DAD WOULD DROP ME OFF...
...BUT HE'S AWAY WORKING IN CALIFORNIA.

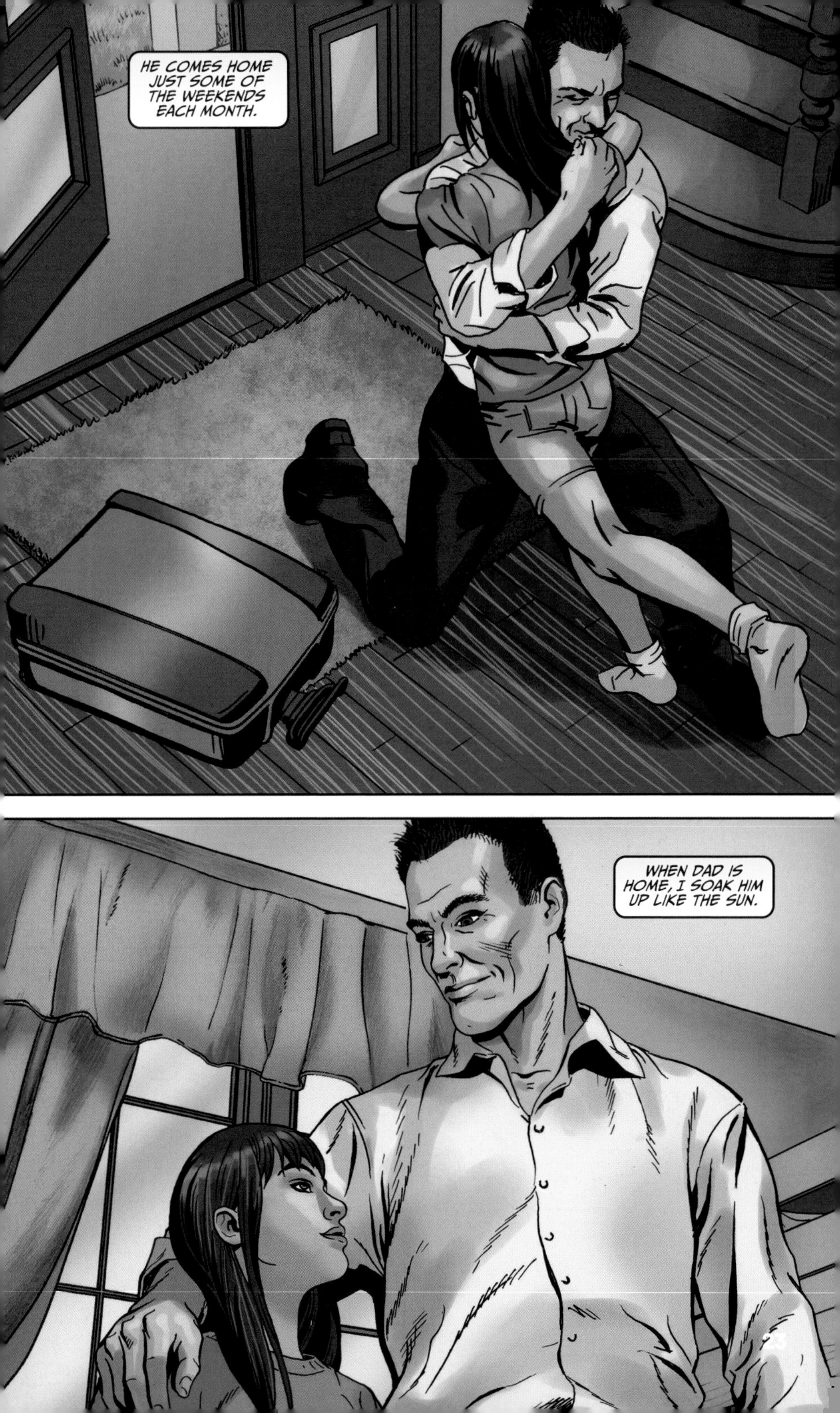
HE COMES HOME JUST SOME OF THE WEEKENDS EACH MONTH.
WHEN DAD IS HOME, I SOAK HIM UP LIKE THE SUN.

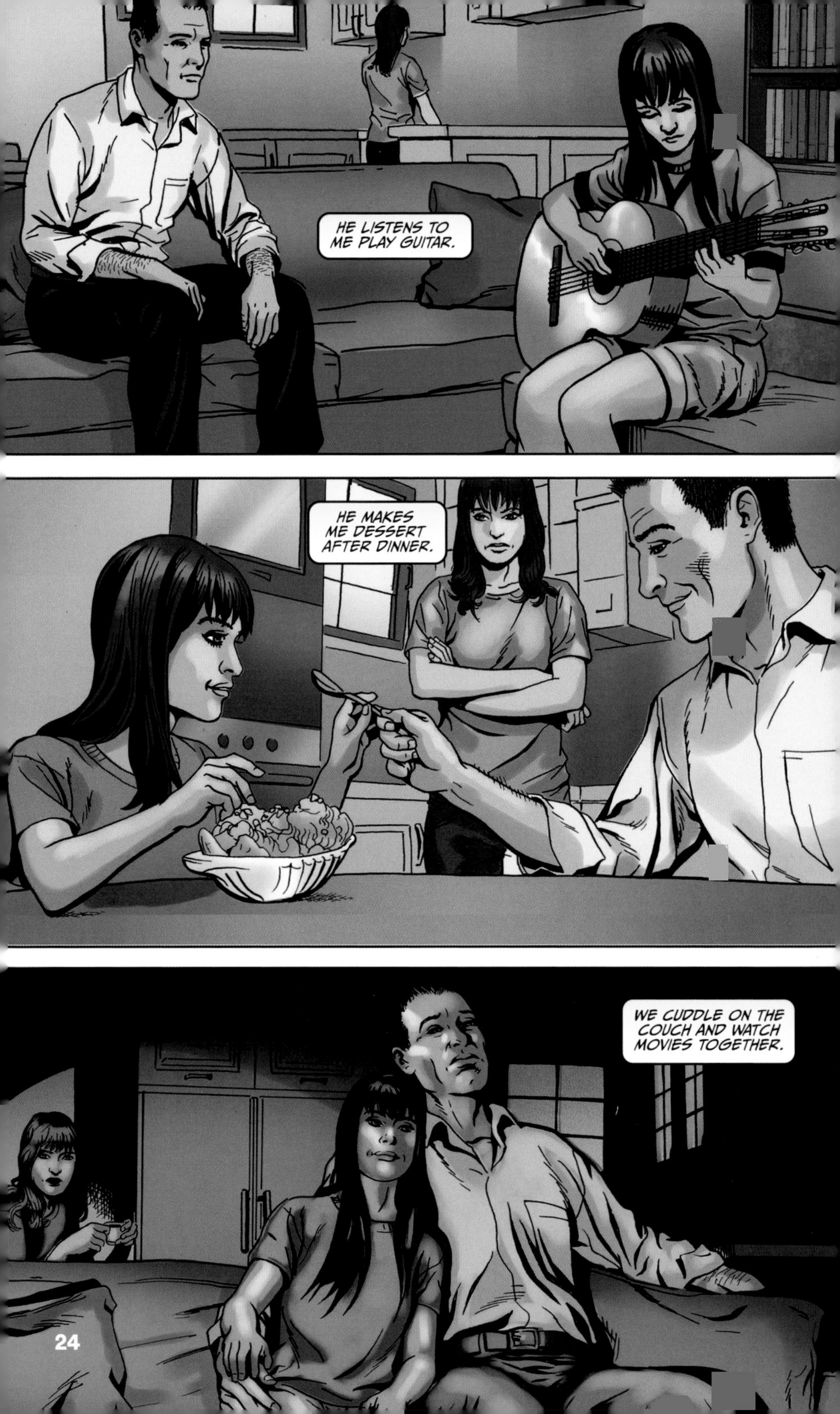
HE LISTENS TO ME PLAY GUITAR.
HE MAKES ME DESSERT AFTER DINNER.
WE CUDDLE ON THE COUCH AND WATCH MOVIES TOGETHER.

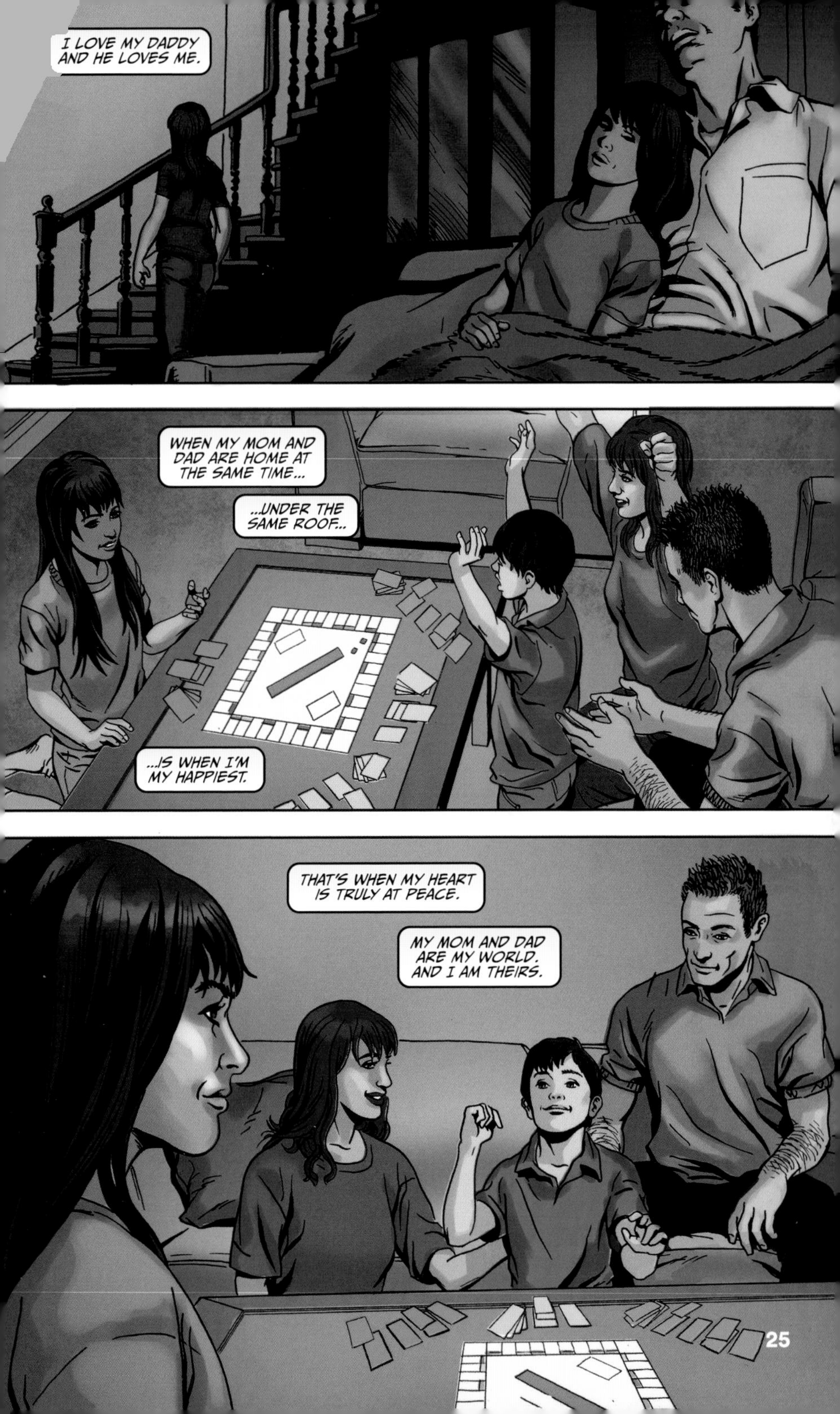
I LOVE MY DADDY AND HE LOVES ME.
WHEN MY MOM AND DAD ARE HOME AT THE SAME TIME...
...UNDER THE SAME ROOF...
...IS WHEN I'M MY HAPPIEST.
THAT'S WHEN MY HEART IS TRULY AT PEACE.
MY MOM AND DAD ARE MY WORLD. AND I AM THEIRS.

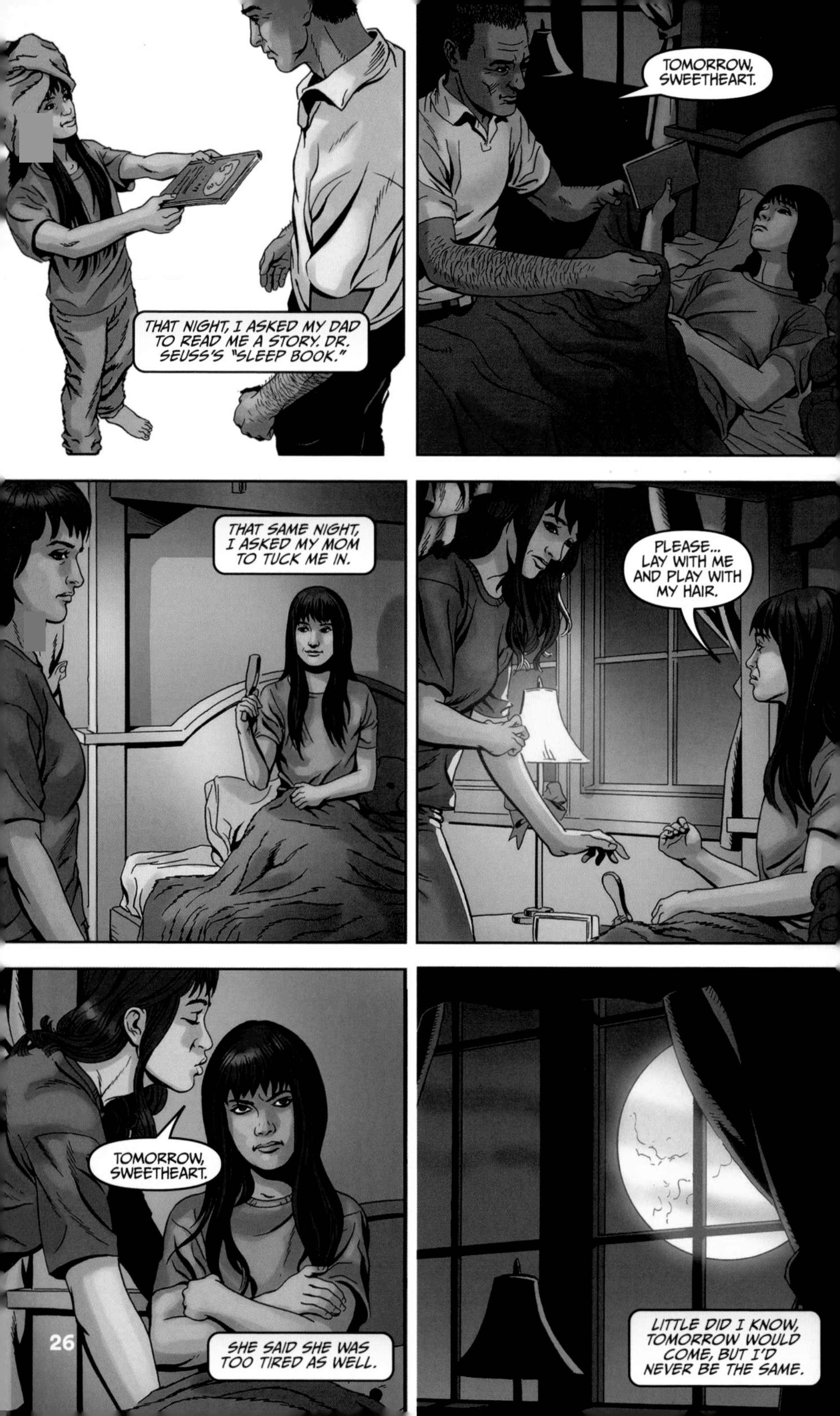
THAT NIGHT, I ASKED MY DAD TO READ ME A STORY. DR. SEUSS'S "SLEEP BOOK."
TOMORROW, SWEETHEART.
THAT SAME NIGHT, I ASKED MY MOM TO TUCK ME IN.
PLEASE... LAY WITH ME AND PLAY WITH MY HAIR.
TOMORROW, SWEETHEART.
SHE SAID SHE WAS TOO TIRED AS WELL.
LITTLE DID I KNOW, TOMORROW WOULD COME, BUT I'D NEVER BE THE SAME.

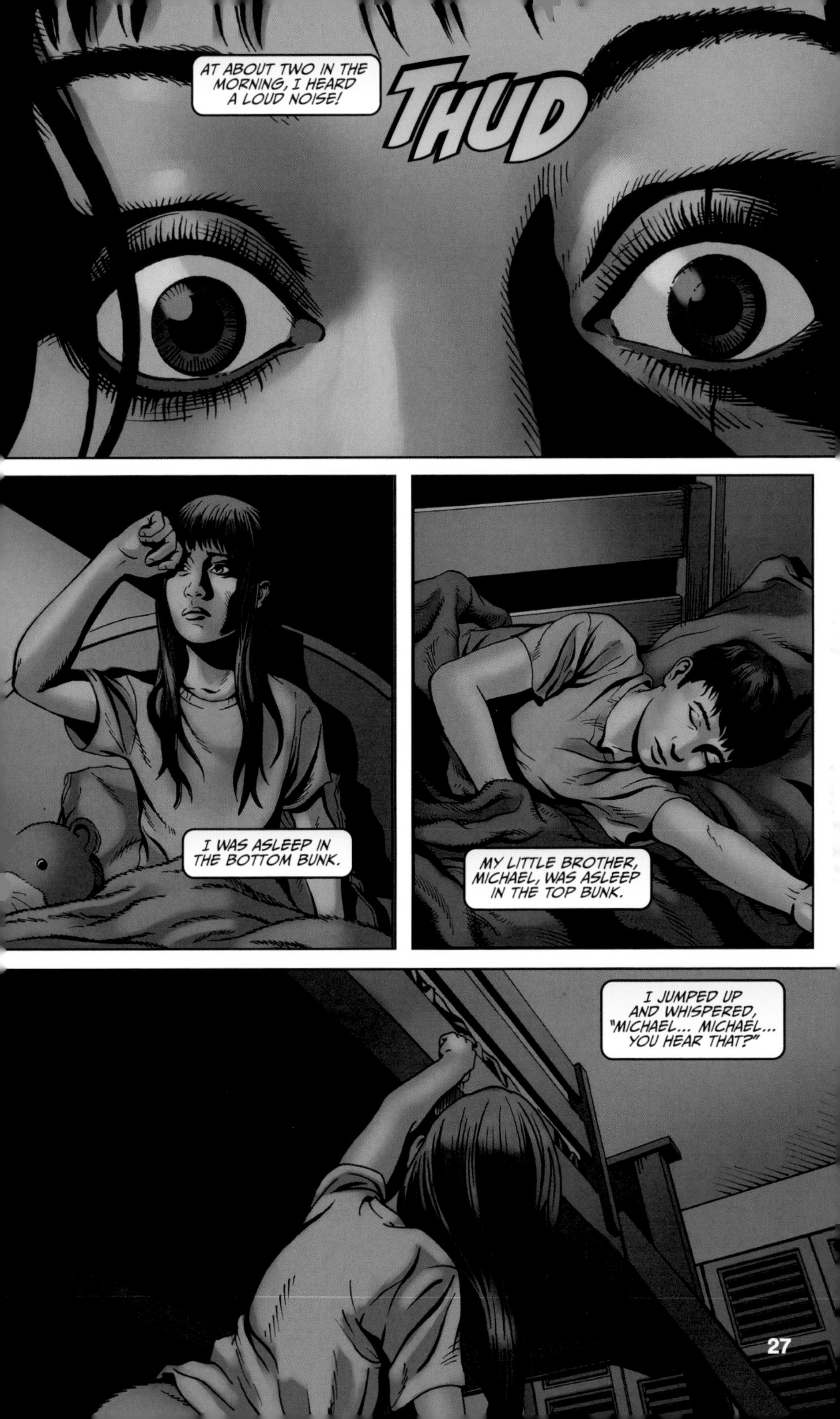
AT ABOUT TWO IN THE MORNING, I HEARD A LOUD NOISE!
THUD
I WAS ASLEEP IN THE BOTTOM BUNK.
MY LITTLE BROTHER, MICHAEL, WAS ASLEEP IN THE TOP BUNK.
I JUMPED UP AND WHISPERED, "MICHAEL... MICHAEL... YOU HEAR THAT?"

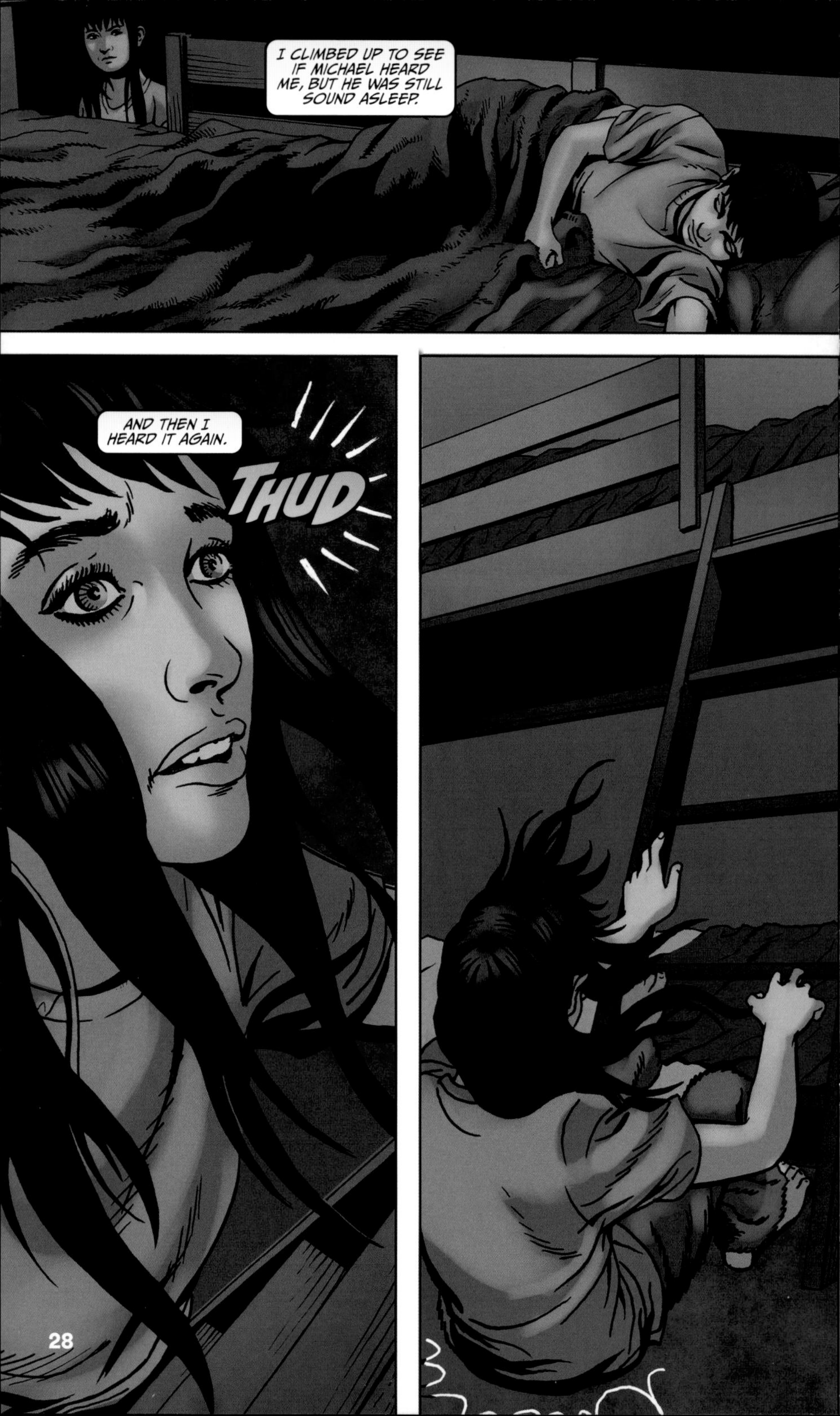
I CLIMBED UP TO SEE IF MICHAEL HEARD ME, BUT HE WAS STILL SOUND ASLEEP.
AND THEN I HEARD IT AGAIN.
THUD

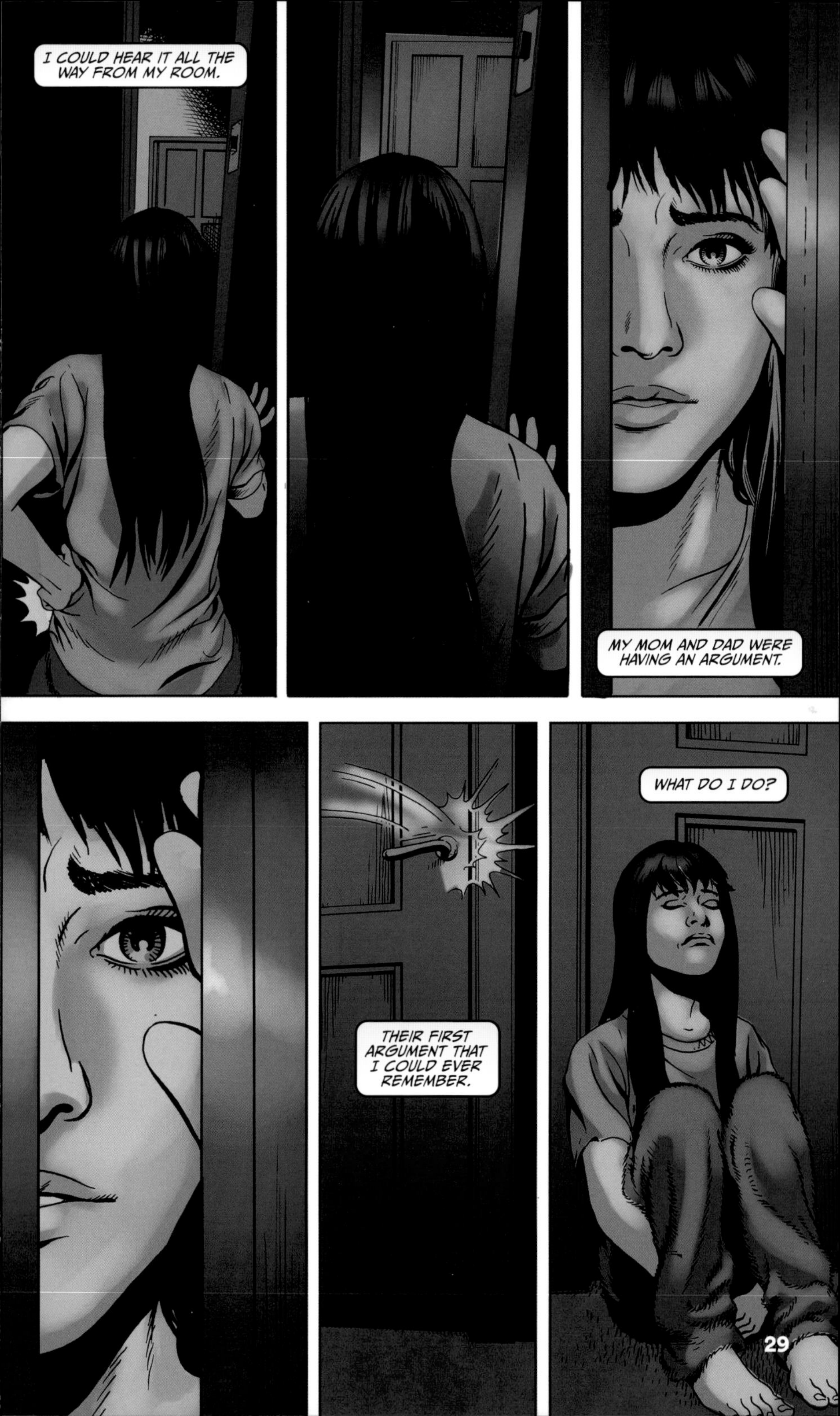
I COULD HEAR IT ALL THE WAY FROM MY ROOM.
MY MOM AND DAD WERE HAVING AN ARGUMENT.
THEIR FIRST ARGUMENT THAT I COULD EVER REMEMBER.
WHAT DO I DO?

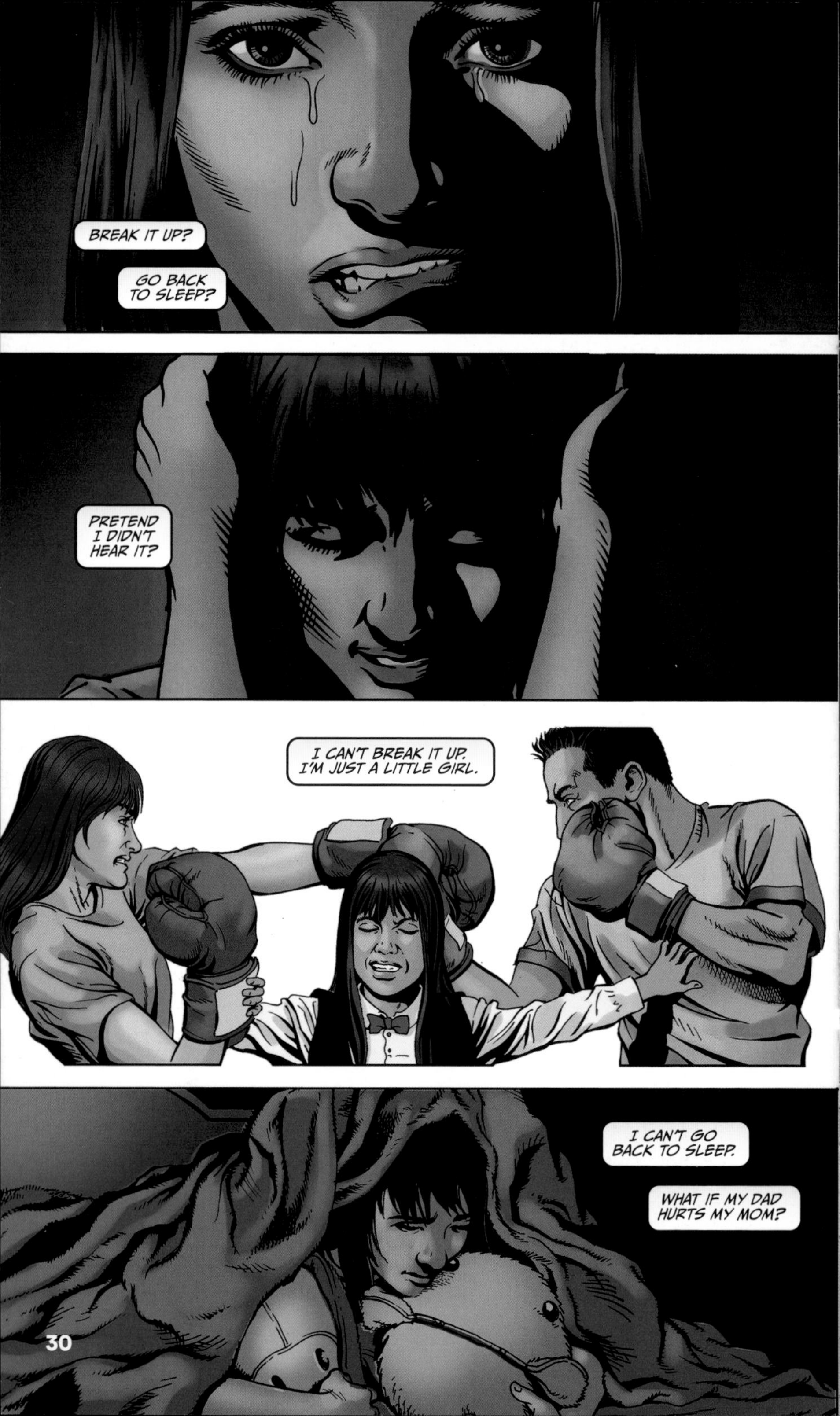
BREAK IT UP?
GO BACK TO SLEEP?
PRETEND I DIDN'T HEAR IT?
I CAN'T BREAK IT UP. I'M JUST A LITTLE GIRL.
I CAN'T GO BACK TO SLEEP.
WHAT IF MY DAD HURTS MY MOM?

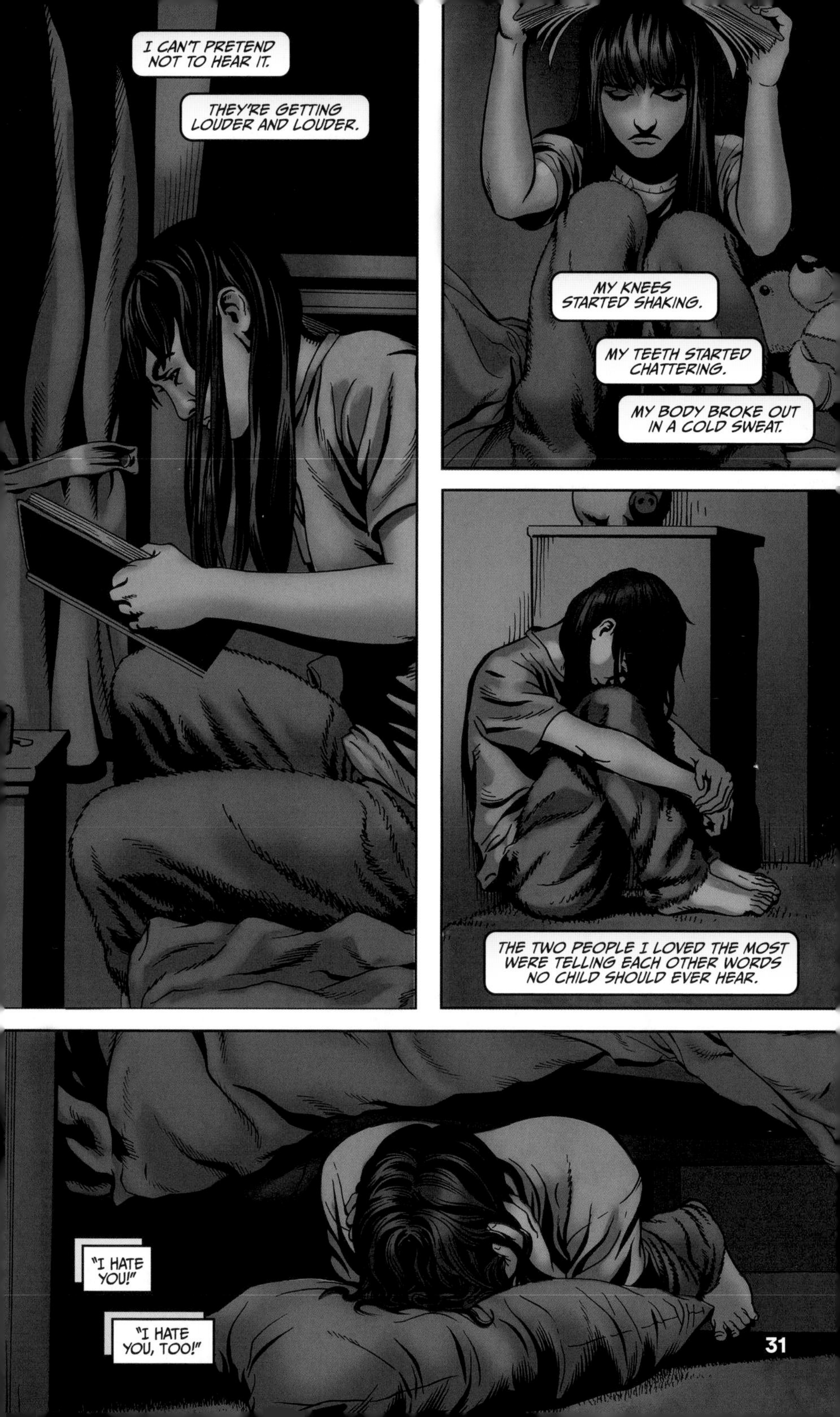
I CAN'T PRETEND NOT TO HEAR IT.
THEY'RE GETTING LOUDER AND LOUDER.
MY KNEES STARTED SHAKING.
MY TEETH STARTED CHATTERING.
MY BODY BROKE OUT IN A COLD SWEAT.
THE TWO PEOPLE I LOVED THE MOST WERE TELLING EACH OTHER WORDS NO CHILD SHOULD EVER HEAR.
"I HATE YOU!"
"I HATE YOU, TOO!"

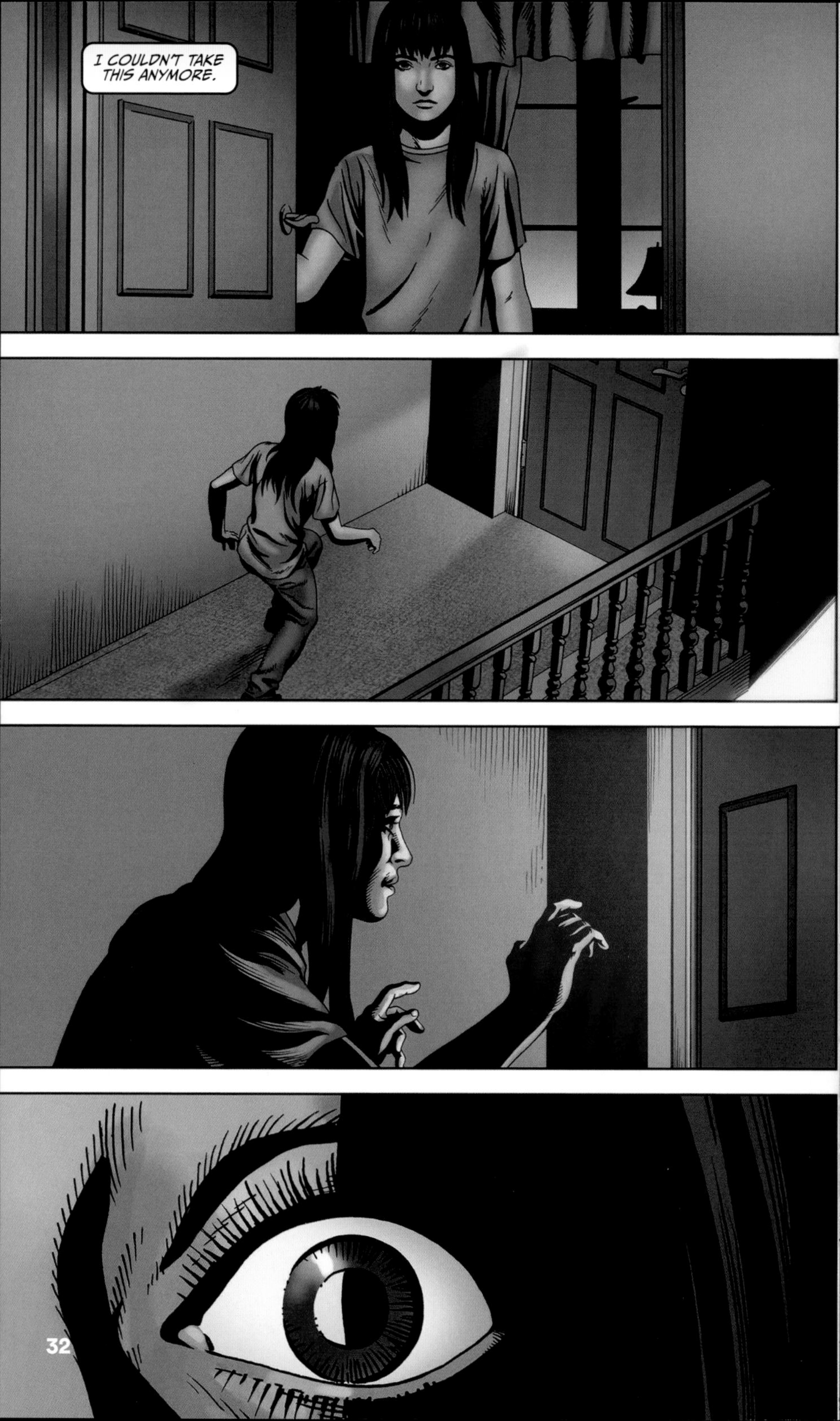
I COULDN'T TAKE THIS ANYMORE.

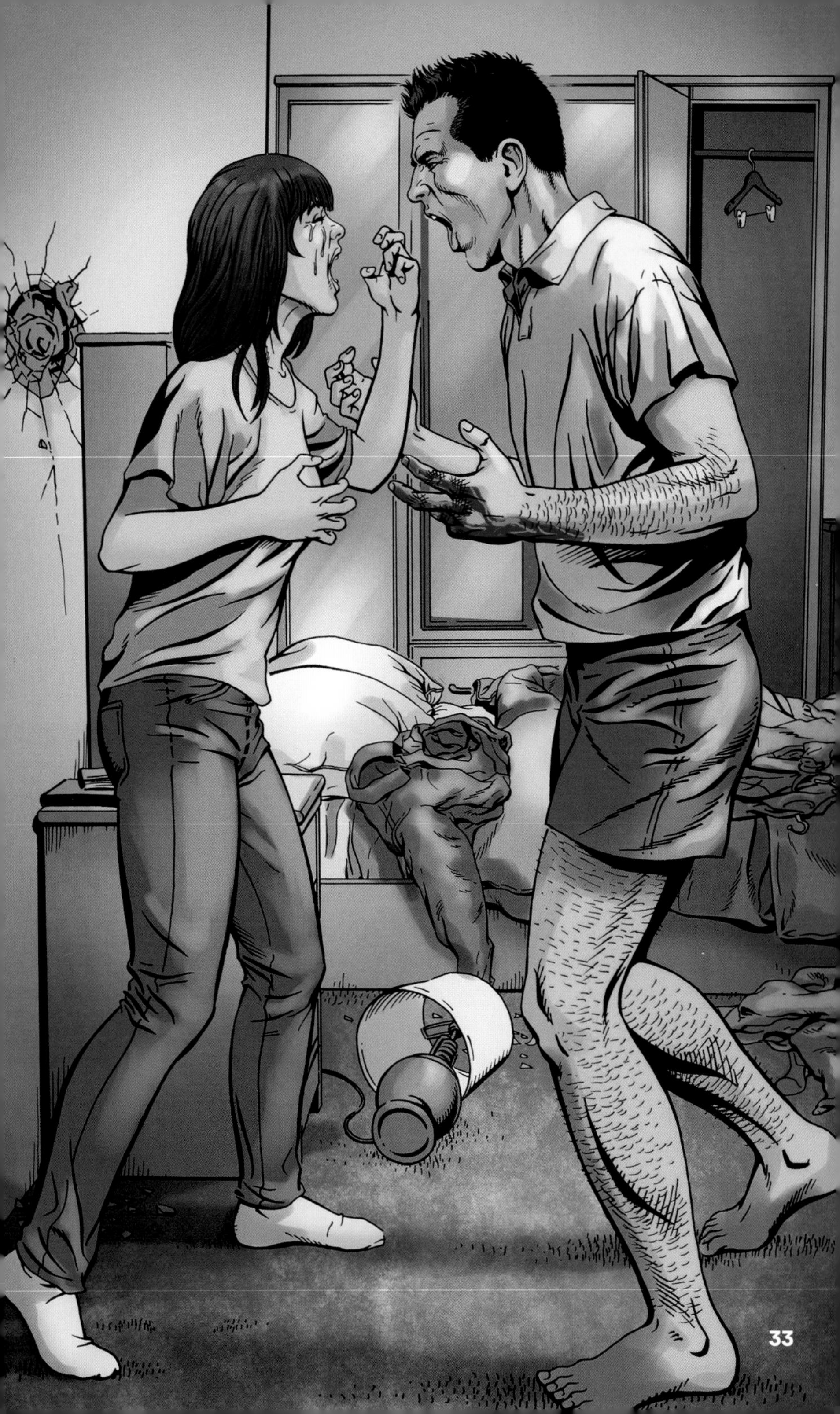

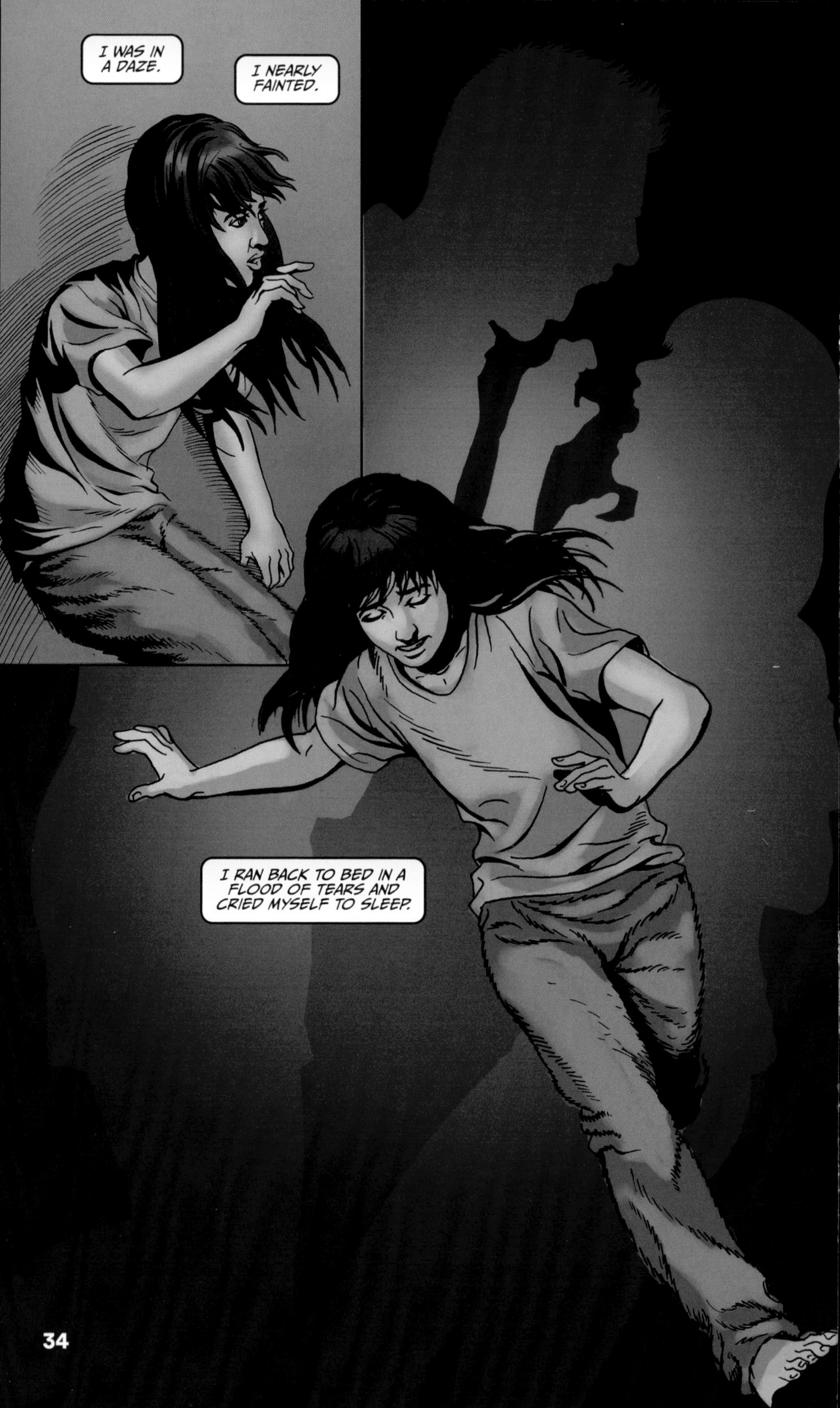
I WAS IN A DAZE.
I NEARLY FAINTED.
I RAN BACK TO BED IN A FLOOD OF TEARS AND CRIED MYSELF TO SLEEP.

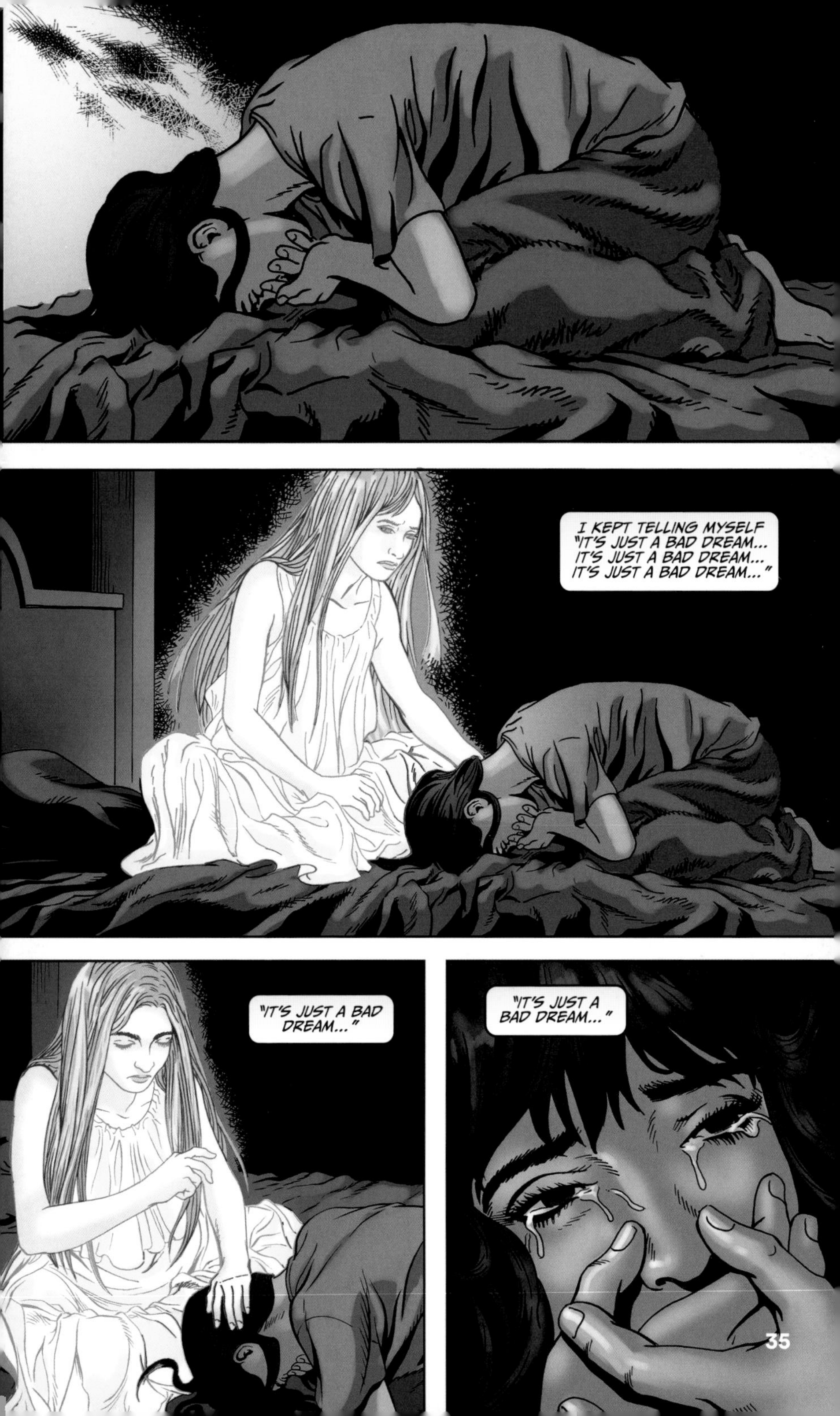
I KEPT TELLING MYSELF "IT'S JUST A BAD DREAM... IT'S JUST A BAD DREAM... IT'S JUST A BAD DREAM..."
"IT'S JUST A BAD DREAM..."
"IT'S JUST A BAD DREAM..."

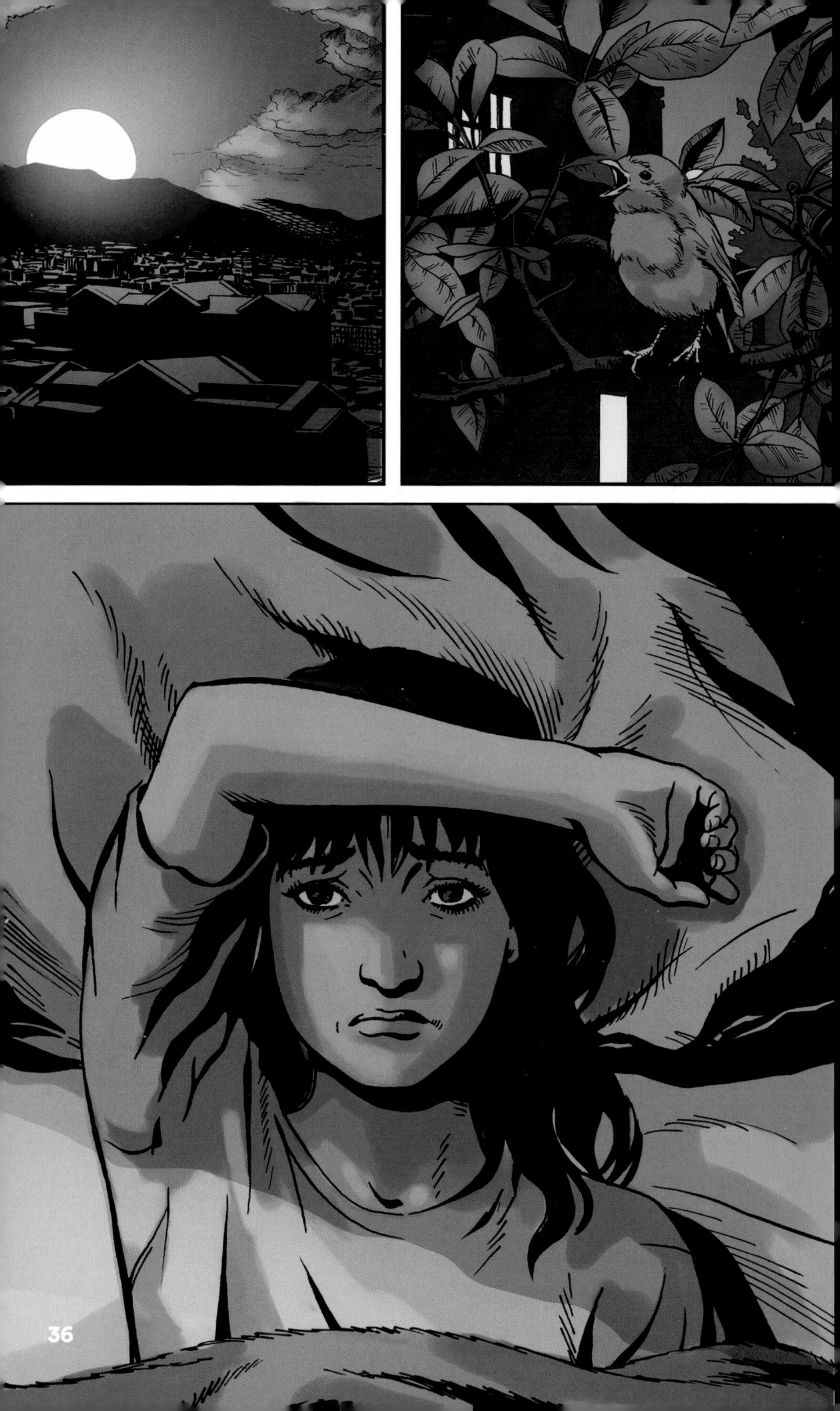

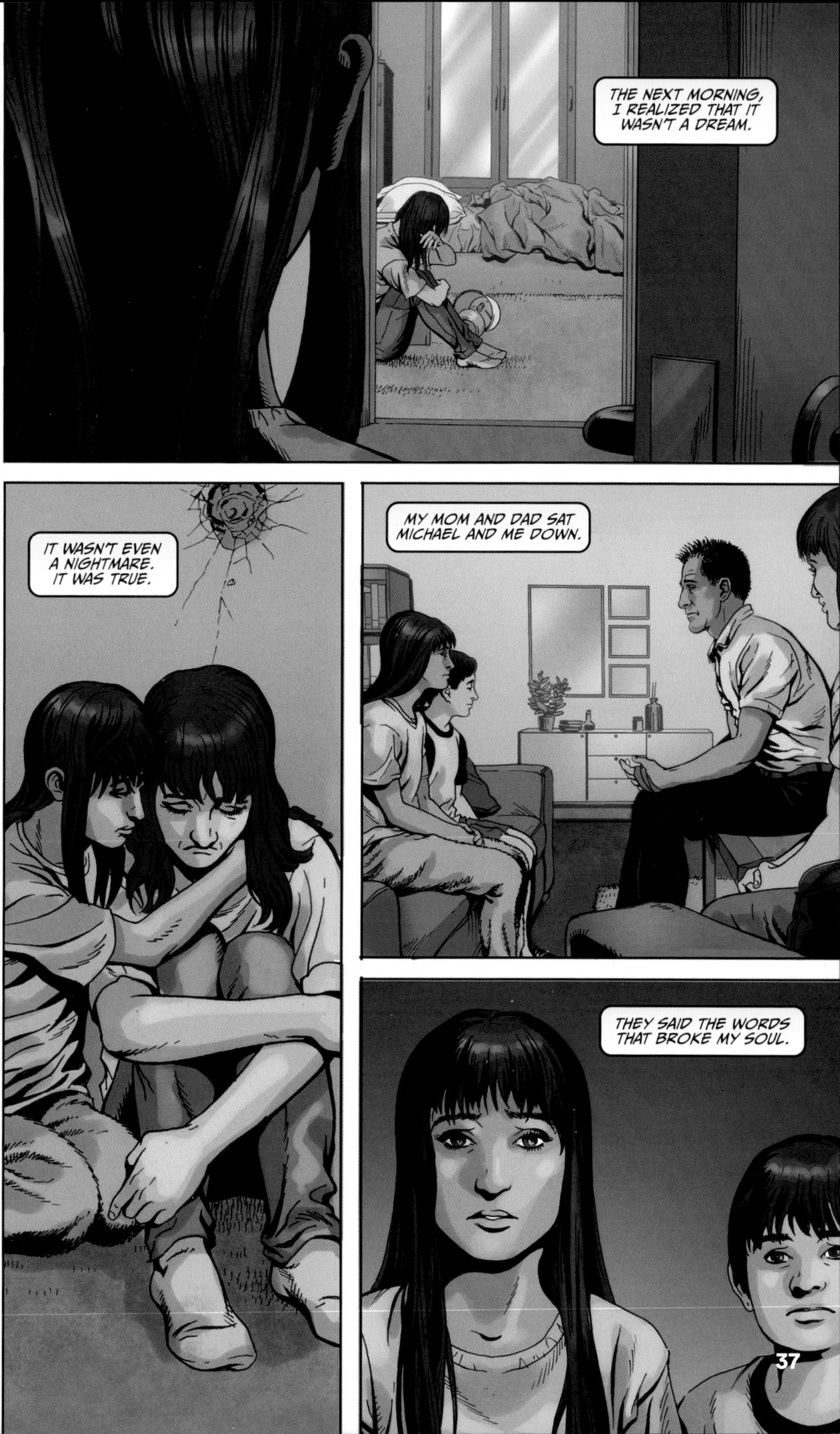
THE NEXT MORNING, I REALIZED THAT IT WASN'T A DREAM.
IT WASN'T EVEN A NIGHTMARE. IT WAS TRUE.
MY MOM AND DAD SAT MICHAEL AND ME DOWN.
THEY SAID THE WORDS THAT BROKE MY SOUL.

WE LOVE YOU GUYS SO MUCH...

BUT WE ARE GETTING A DIVORCE.

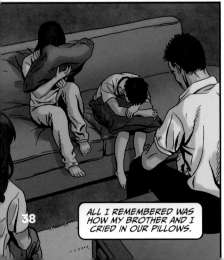

ALL I REMEMBERED WAS HOW MY BROTHER AND I CRIED IN OUR PILLOWS.

WHAT DOES THIS MEAN?

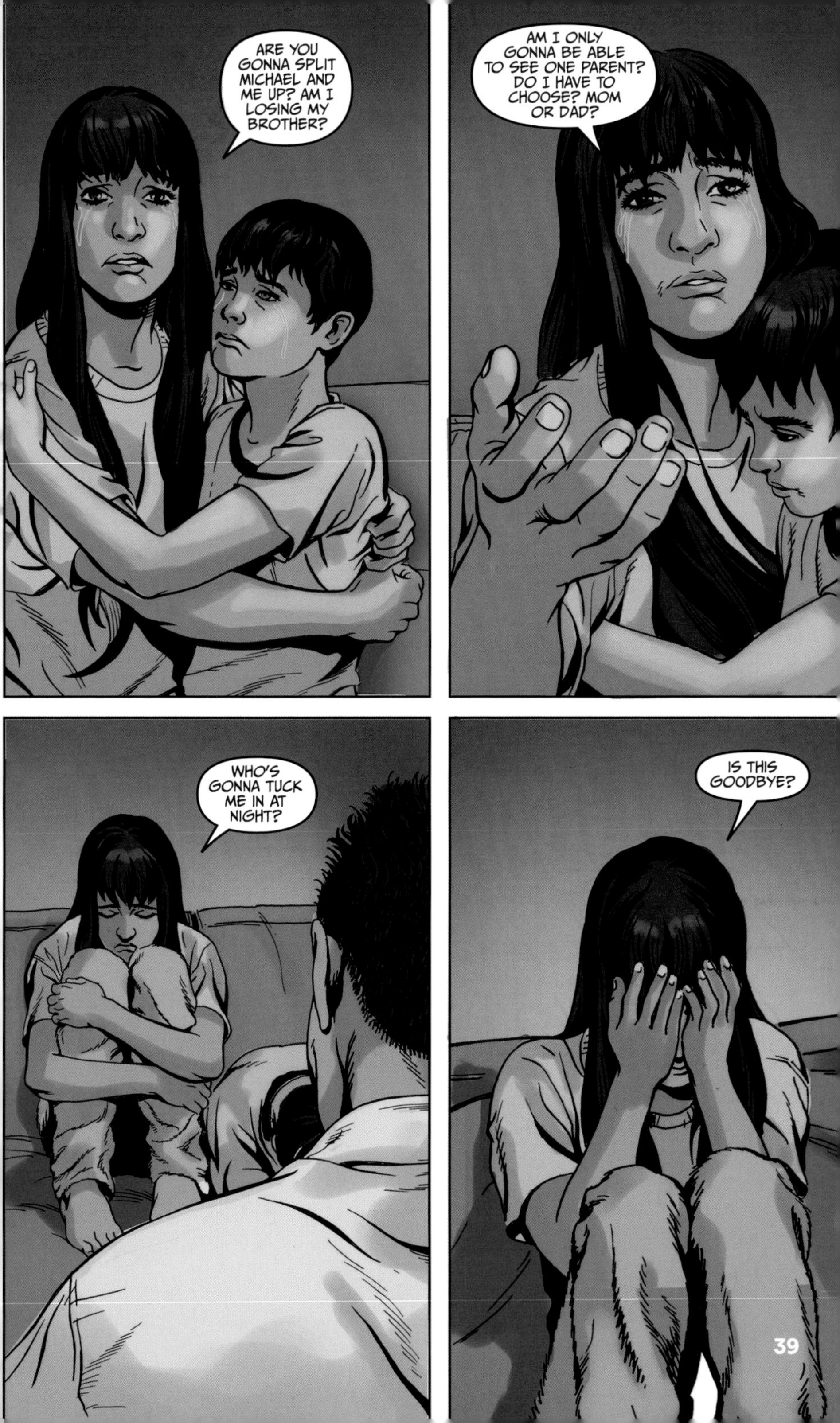
ARE YOU GONNA SPLIT MICHAEL AND ME UP? AM I LOSING MY BROTHER?
AM I ONLY GONNA BE ABLE TO SEE ONE PARENT? DO I HAVE TO CHOOSE? MOM OR DAD?
WHO'S GONNA TUCK ME IN AT NIGHT?
IS THIS GOODBYE?

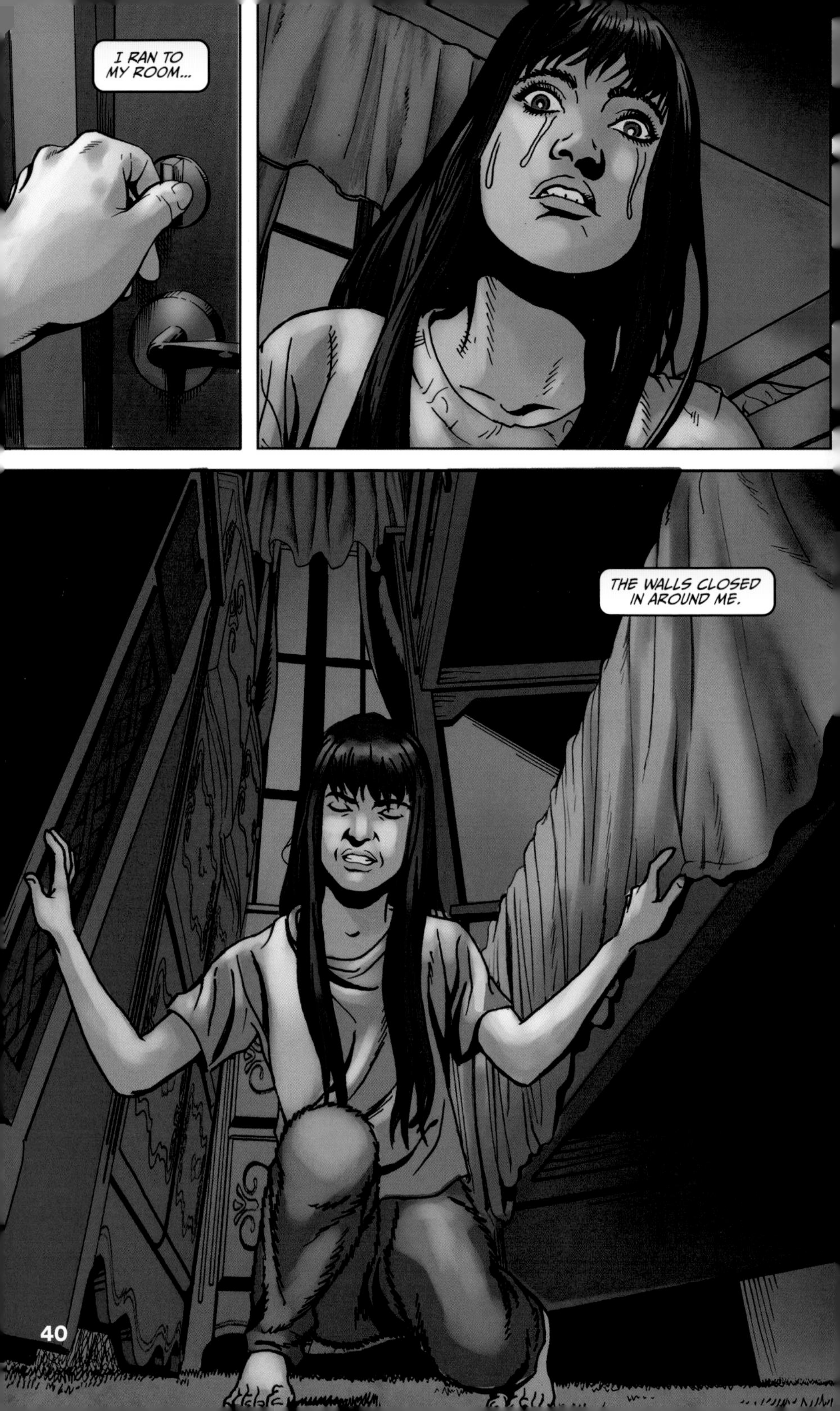
I RAN TO MY ROOM...
THE WALLS CLOSED IN AROUND ME.

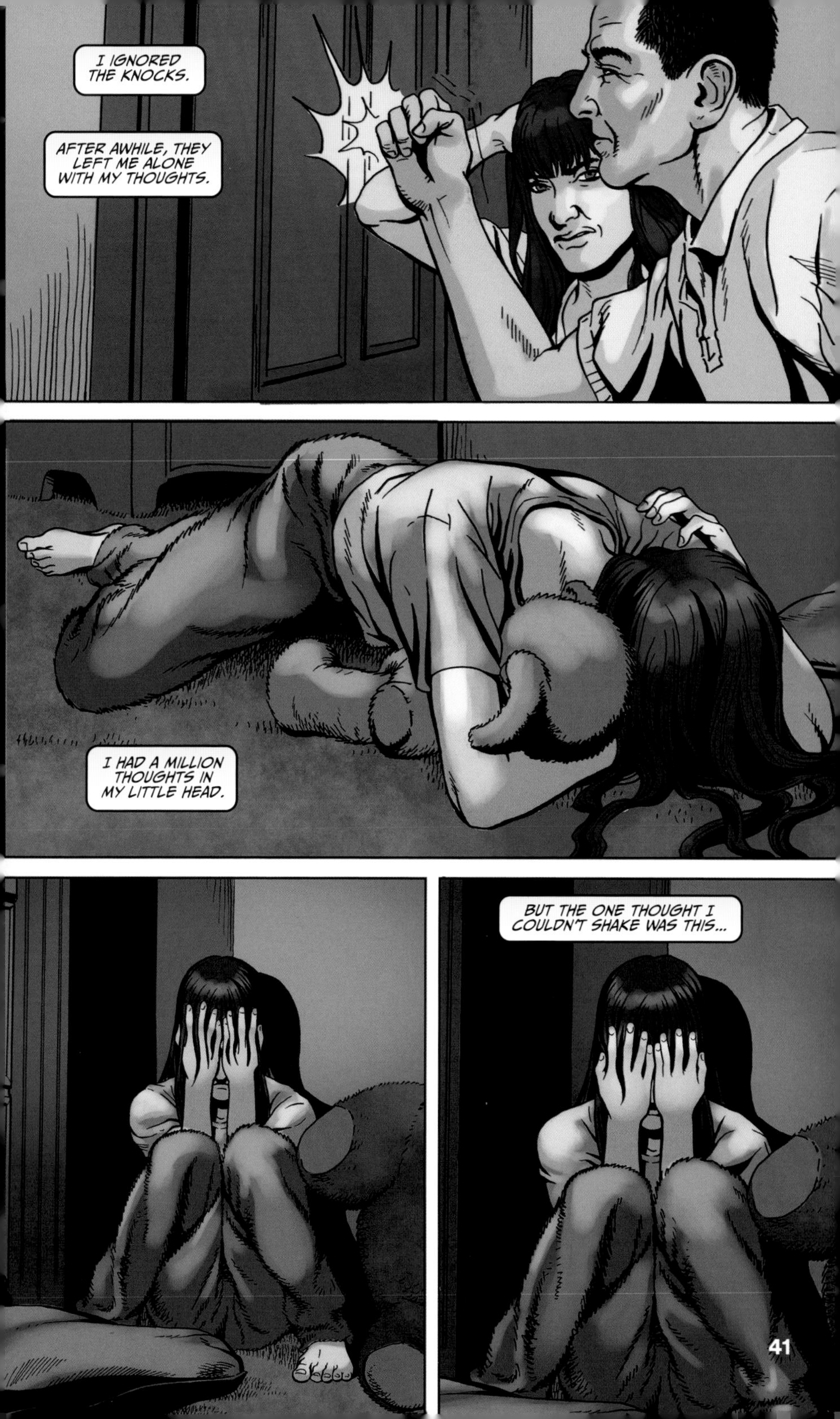
I IGNORED THE KNOCKS.
AFTER AWHILE, THEY LEFT ME ALONE WITH MY THOUGHTS.
I HAD A MILLION THOUGHTS IN MY LITTLE HEAD.
BUT THE ONE THOUGHT I COULDN'T SHAKE WAS THIS...

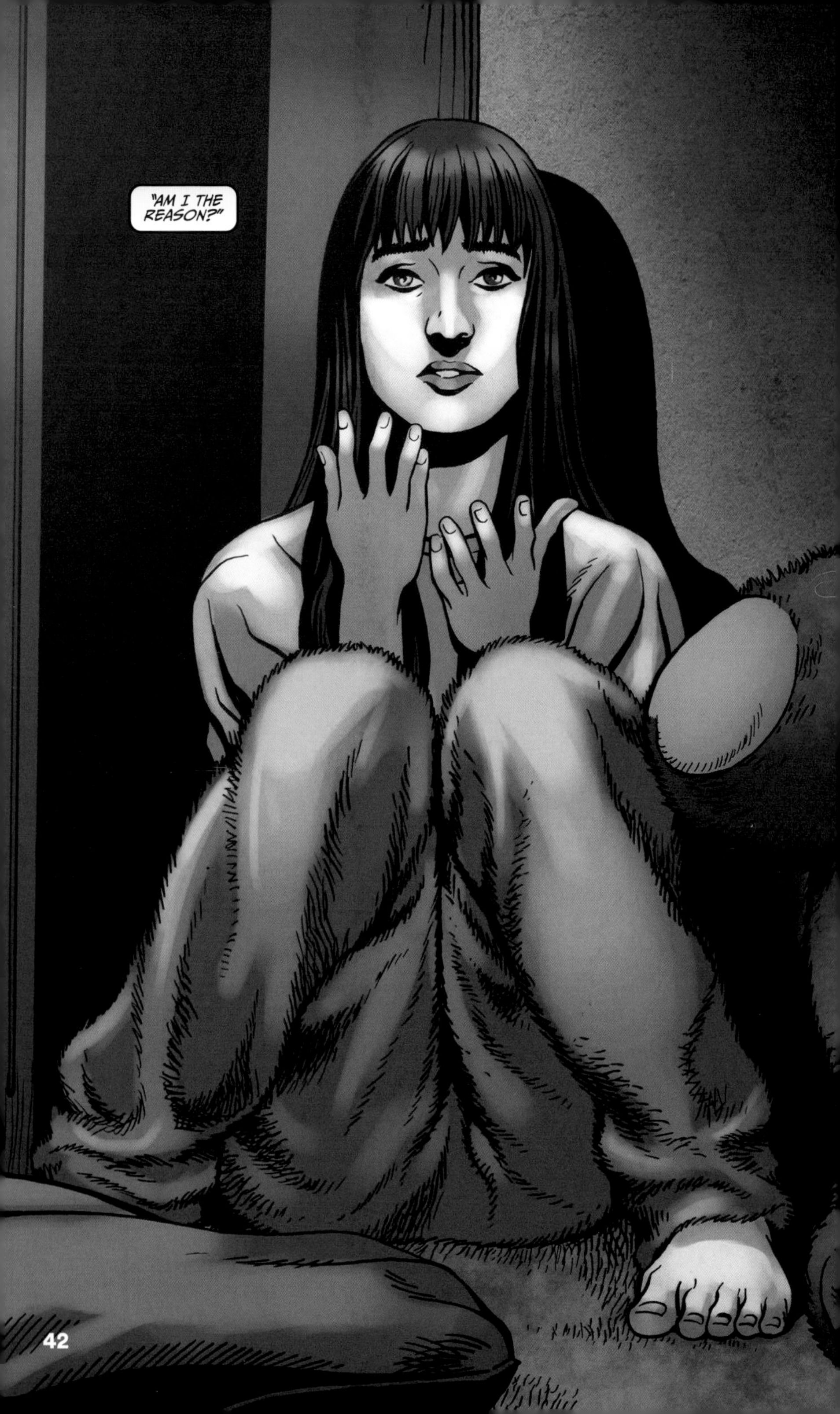
"AM I THE REASON?"

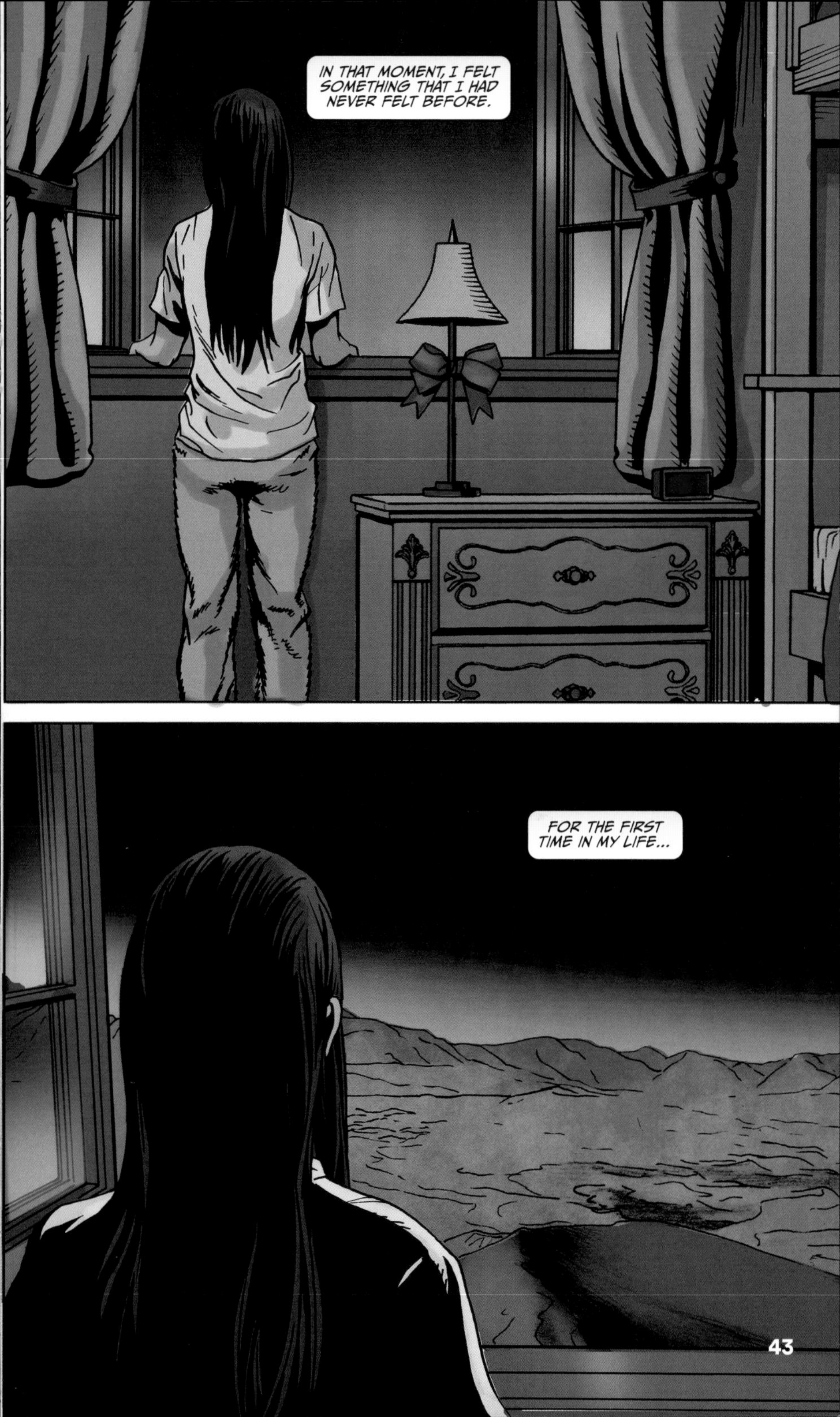
IN THAT MOMENT, I FELT SOMETHING THAT I HAD NEVER FELT BEFORE.
FOR THE FIRST TIME IN MY LIFE...

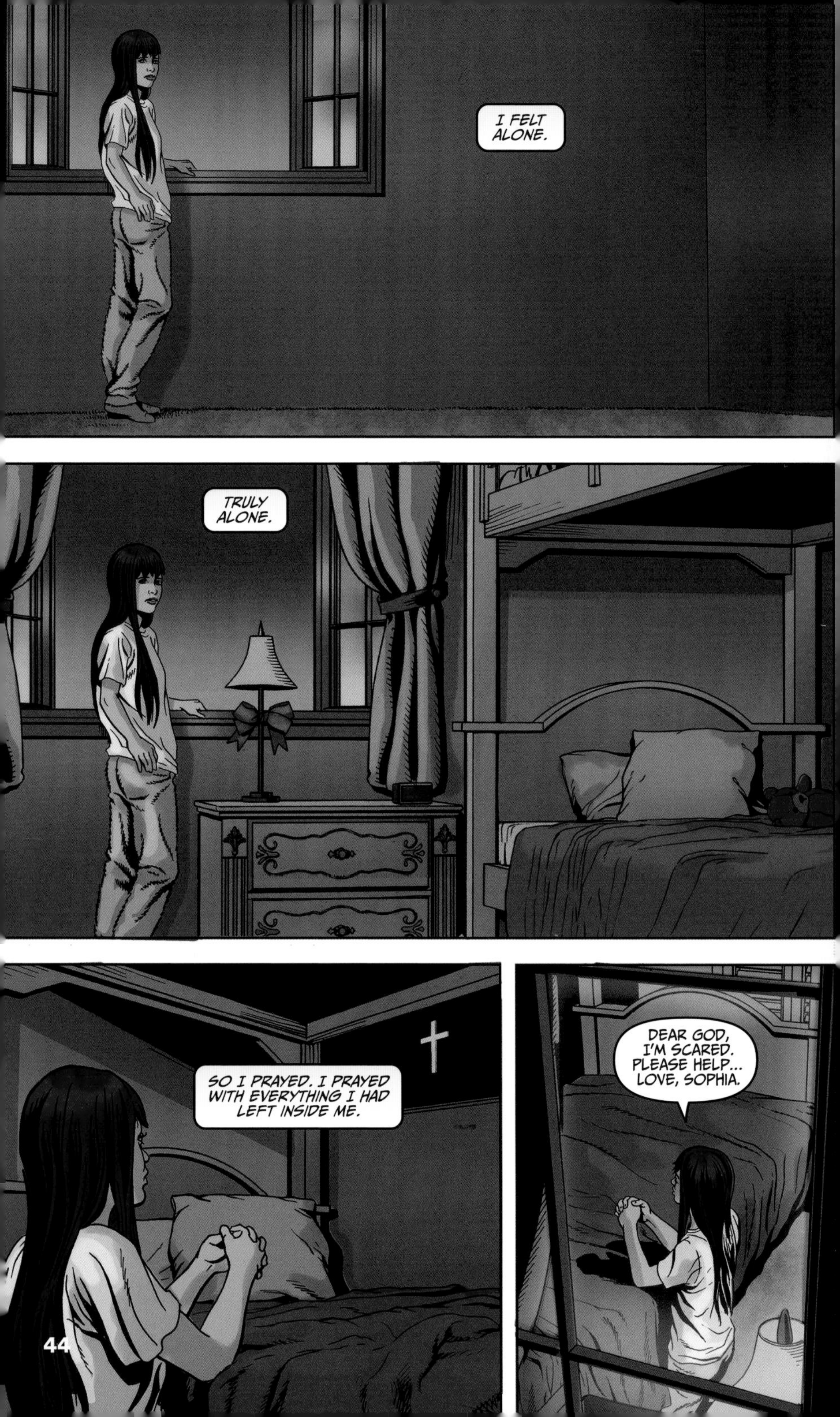
I FELT ALONE.
TRULY ALONE.
SO I PRAYED. I PRAYED WITH EVERYTHING I HAD LEFT INSIDE ME.
DEAR GOD, I'M SCARED. PLEASE HELP... LOVE, SOPHIA.

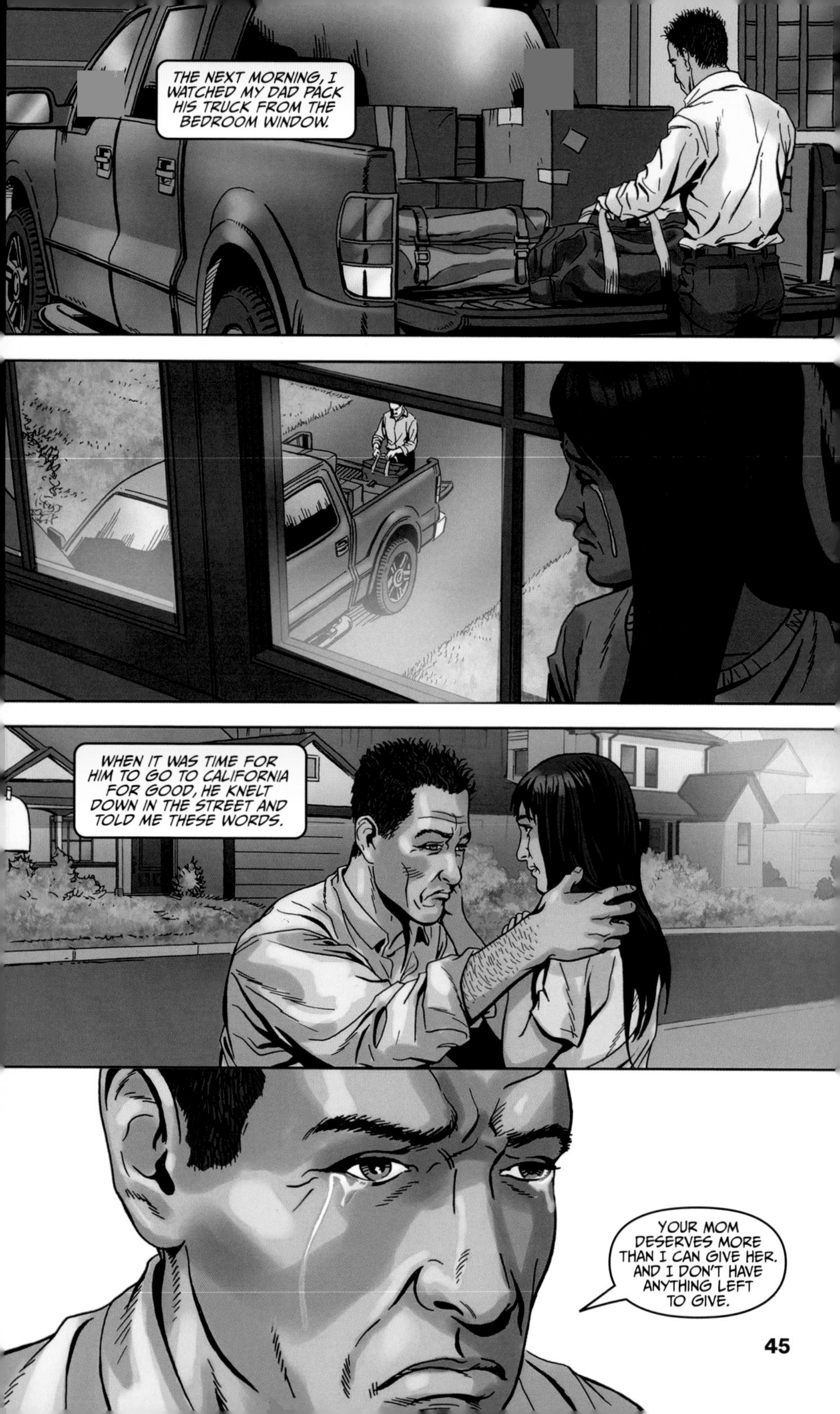
THE NEXT MORNING, I WATCHED MY DAD PACK HIS TRUCK FROM THE BEDROOM WINDOW.
WHEN IT WAS TIME FOR HIM TO GO TO CALIFORNIA FOR GOOD, HE KNELT DOWN IN THE STREET AND TOLD ME THESE WORDS.
YOUR MOM DESERVES MORE THAN I CAN GIVE HER. AND I DON'T HAVE ANYTHING LEFT TO GIVE.

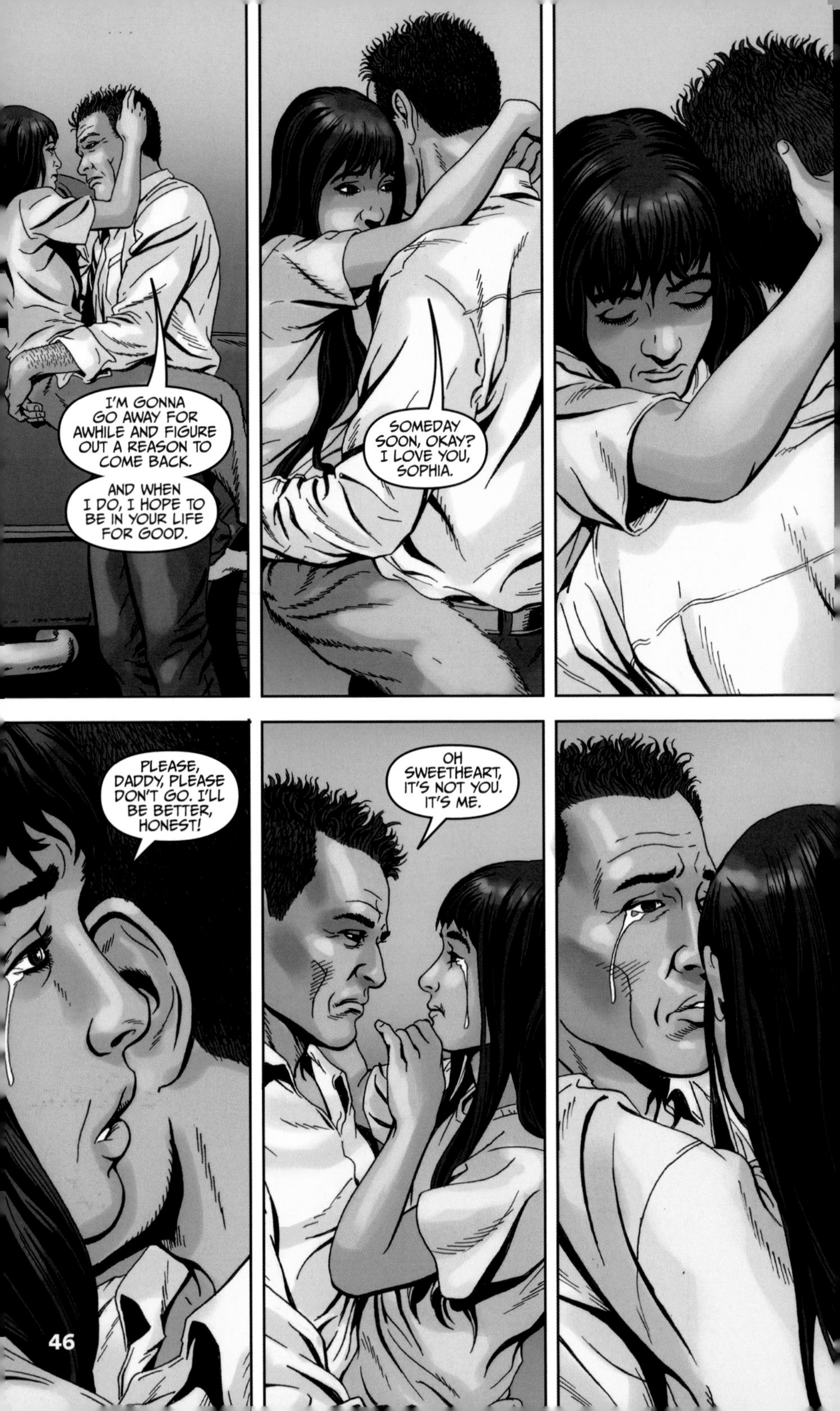
I'M GONNA GO AWAY FOR AWHILE AND FIGURE OUT A REASON TO COME BACK.
AND WHEN I DO, I HOPE TO BE IN YOUR LIFE FOR GOOD.
SOMEDAY SOON, OKAY? I LOVE YOU, SOPHIA.
PLEASE, DADDY, PLEASE DON'T GO. I'LL BE BETTER, HONEST!
OH SWEETHEART, IT'S NOT YOU. IT'S ME.

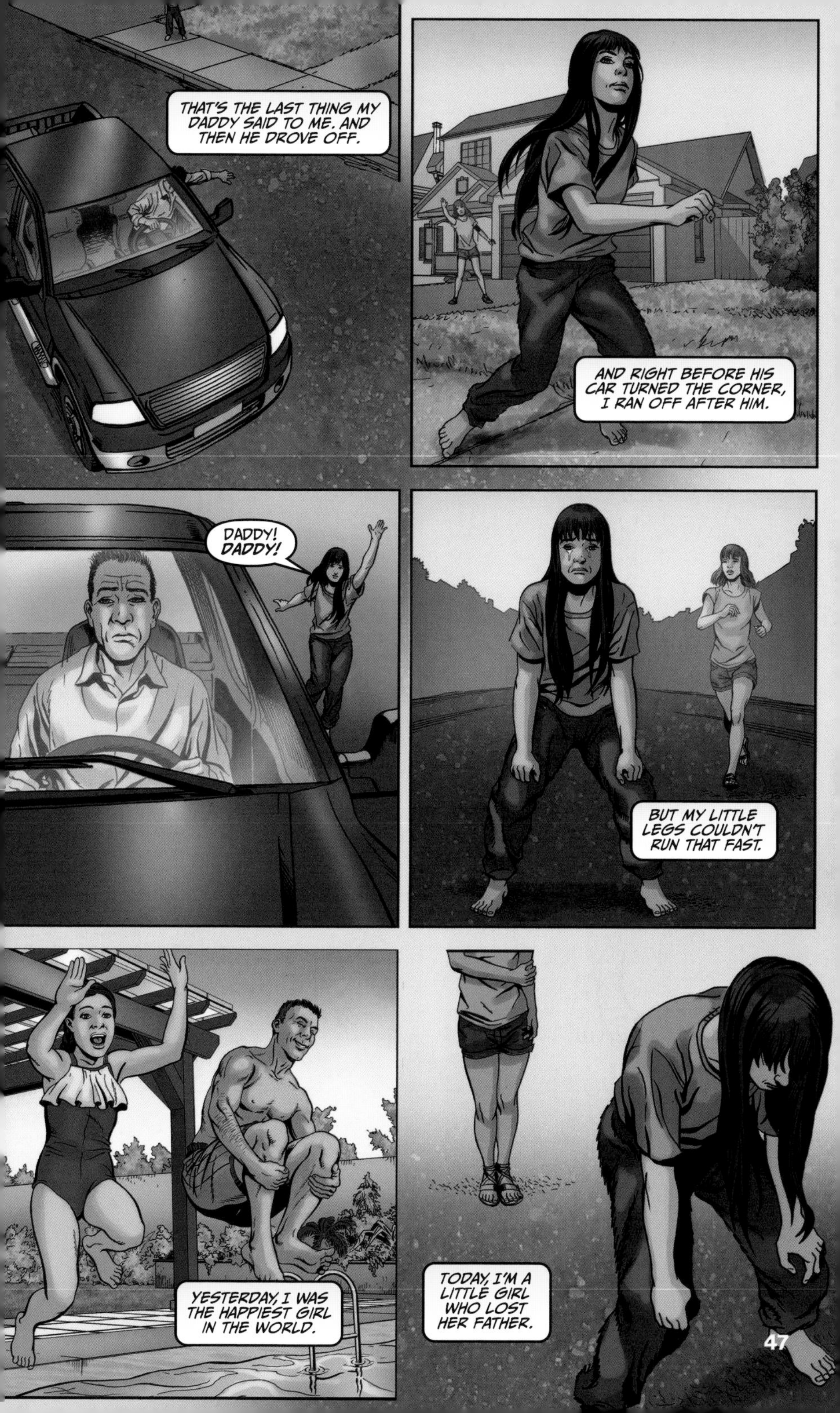

THAT'S THE LAST THING MY DADDY SAID TO ME. AND THEN HE DROVE OFF.
AND RIGHT BEFORE HIS CAR TURNED THE CORNER, I RAN OFF AFTER HIM.
DADDY! DADDY!
BUT MY LITTLE LEGS COULDN'T RUN THAT FAST.
YESTERDAY, I WAS THE HAPPIEST GIRL IN THE WORLD.
TODAY, I'M A LITTLE GIRL WHO LOST HER FATHER.

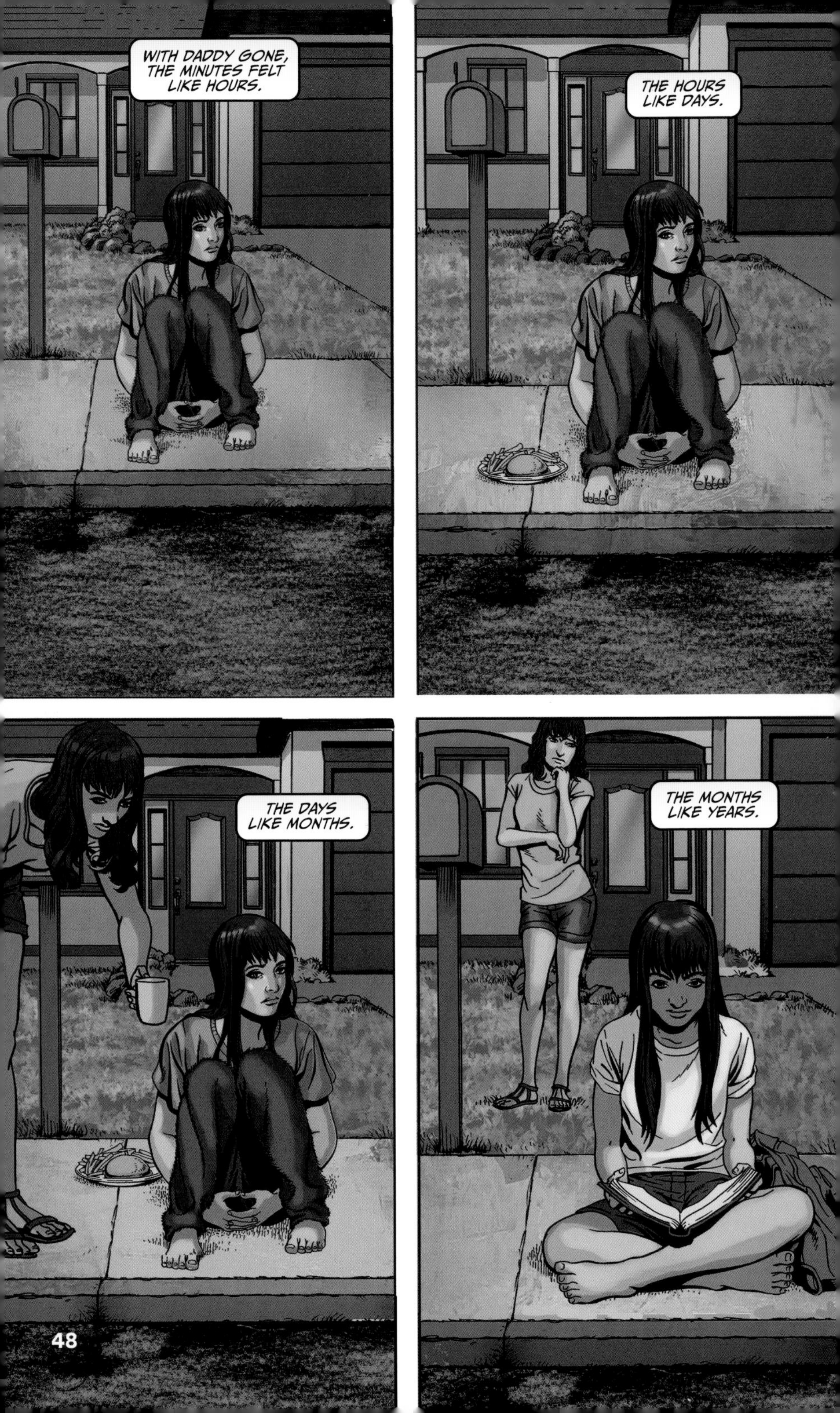
WITH DADDY GONE, THE MINUTES FELT LIKE HOURS.
THE HOURS LIKE DAYS.
THE DAYS LIKE MONTHS.
THE MONTHS LIKE YEARS.

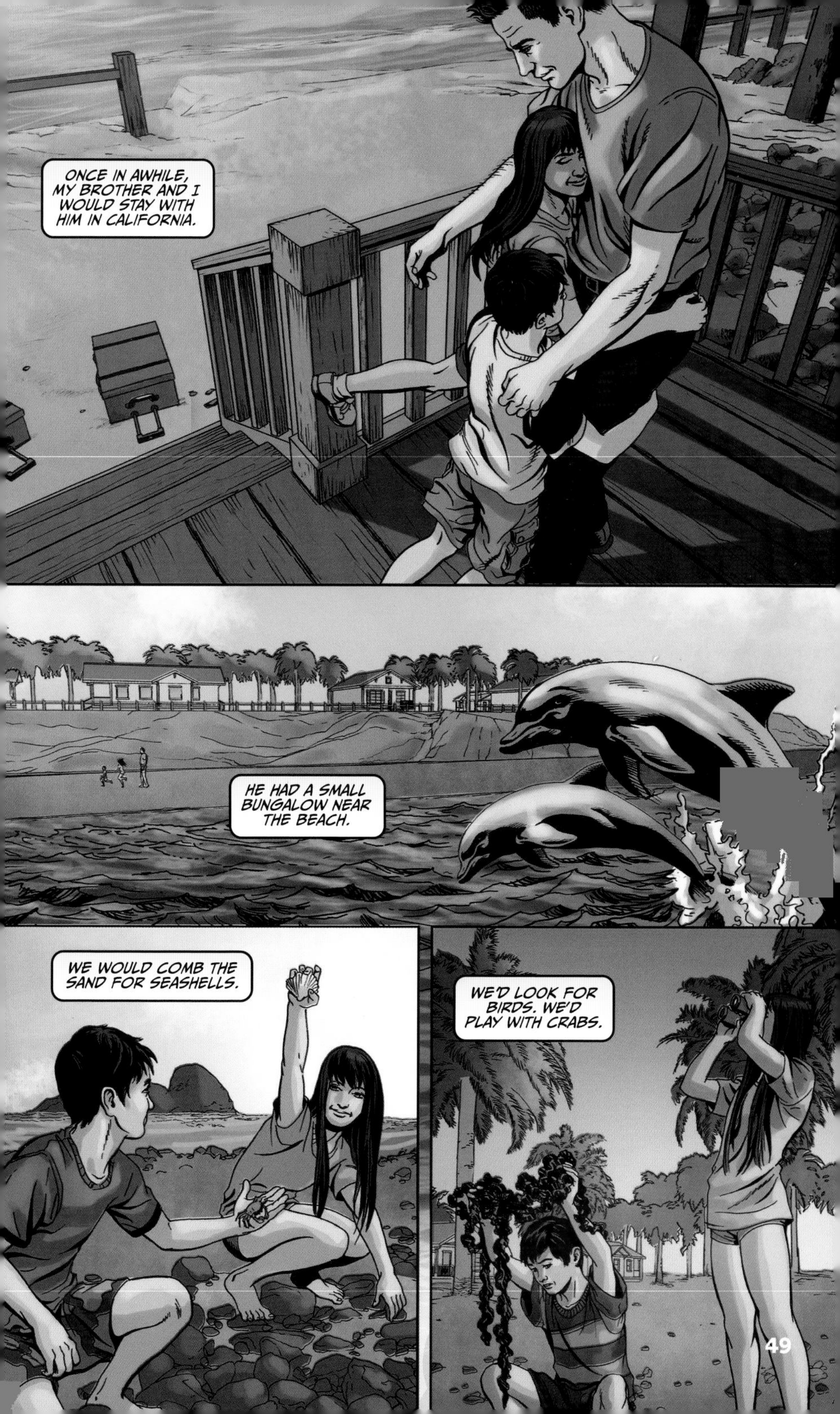
ONCE IN AWHILE, MY BROTHER AND I WOULD STAY WITH HIM IN CALIFORNIA.
HE HAD A SMALL BUNGALOW NEAR THE BEACH.
WE WOULD COMB THE SAND FOR SEASHELLS.
WE'D LOOK FOR BIRDS. WE'D PLAY WITH CRABS.

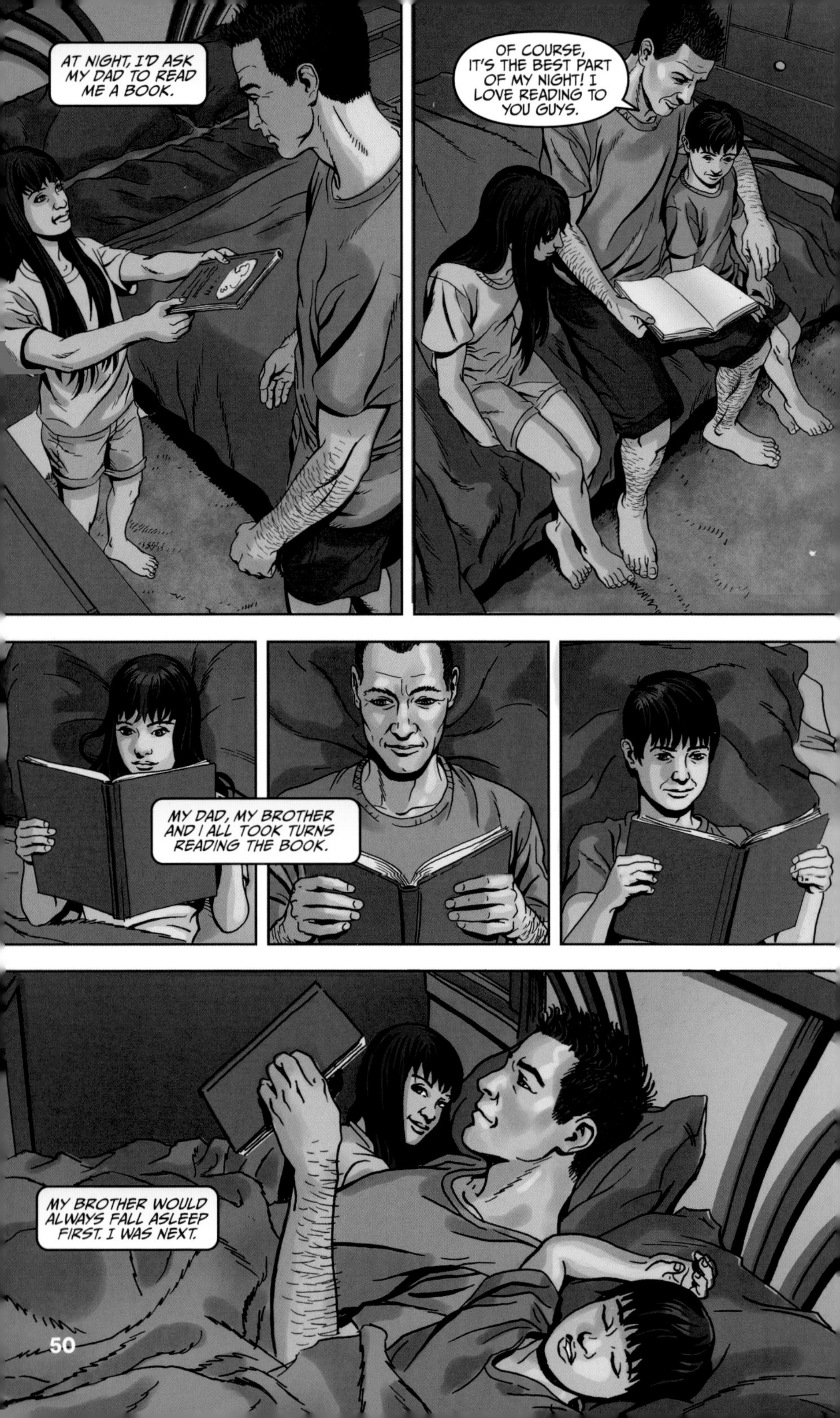
AT NIGHT, I'D ASK MY DAD TO READ ME A BOOK.
OF COURSE, IT'S THE BEST PART OF MY NIGHT! I LOVE READING TO YOU GUYS.
MY DAD, MY BROTHER AND I ALL TOOK TURNS READING THE BOOK.
MY BROTHER WOULD ALWAYS FALL ASLEEP FIRST. I WAS NEXT.

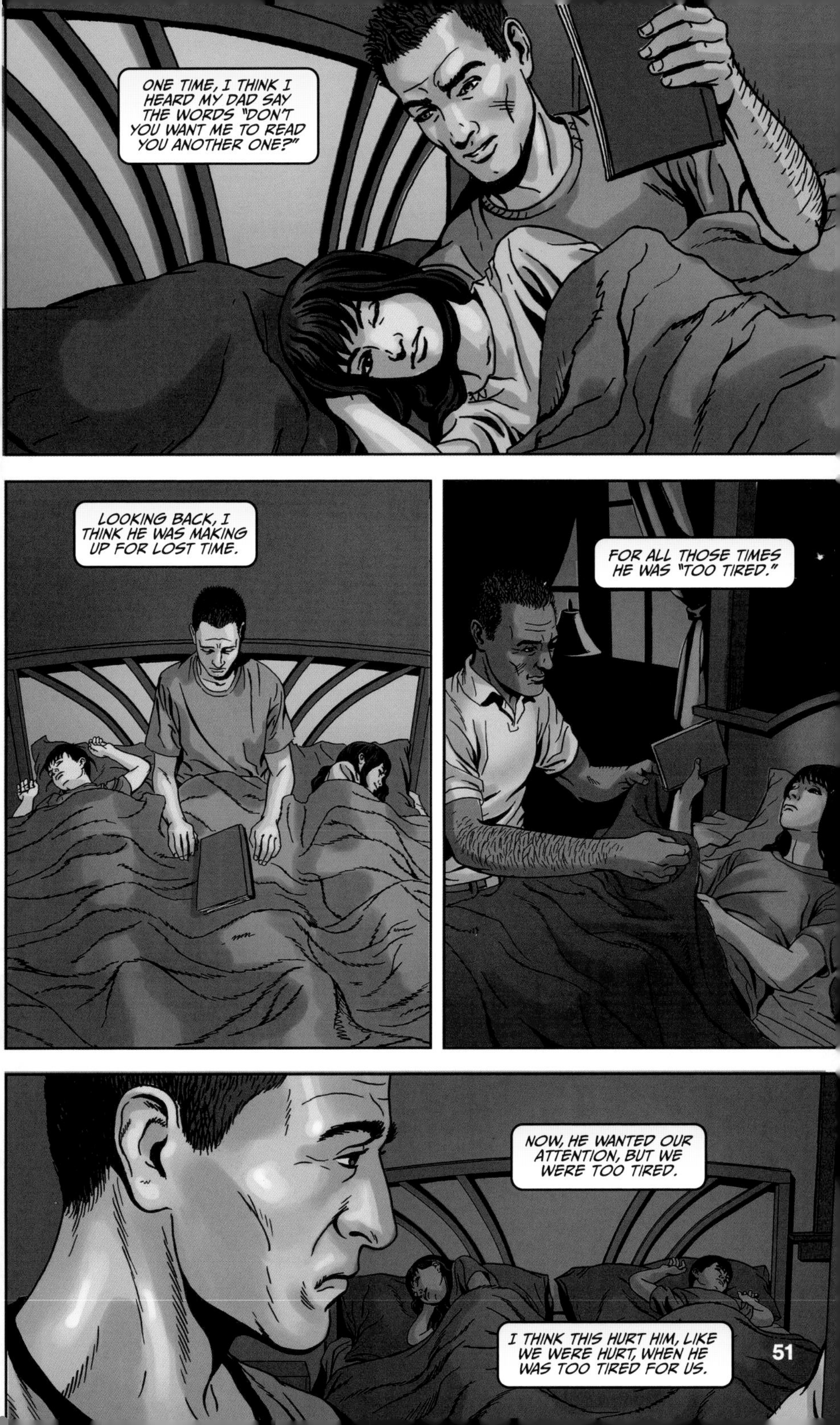
ONE TIME, I THINK I HEARD MY DAD SAY THE WORDS "DON'T YOU WANT ME TO READ YOU ANOTHER ONE?"
LOOKING BACK, I THINK HE WAS MAKING UP FOR LOST TIME.
FOR ALL THOSE TIMES HE WAS "TOO TIRED."
NOW, HE WANTED OUR ATTENTION, BUT WE WERE TOO TIRED.
I THINK THIS HURT HIM, LIKE WE WERE HURT, WHEN HE WAS TOO TIRED FOR US.

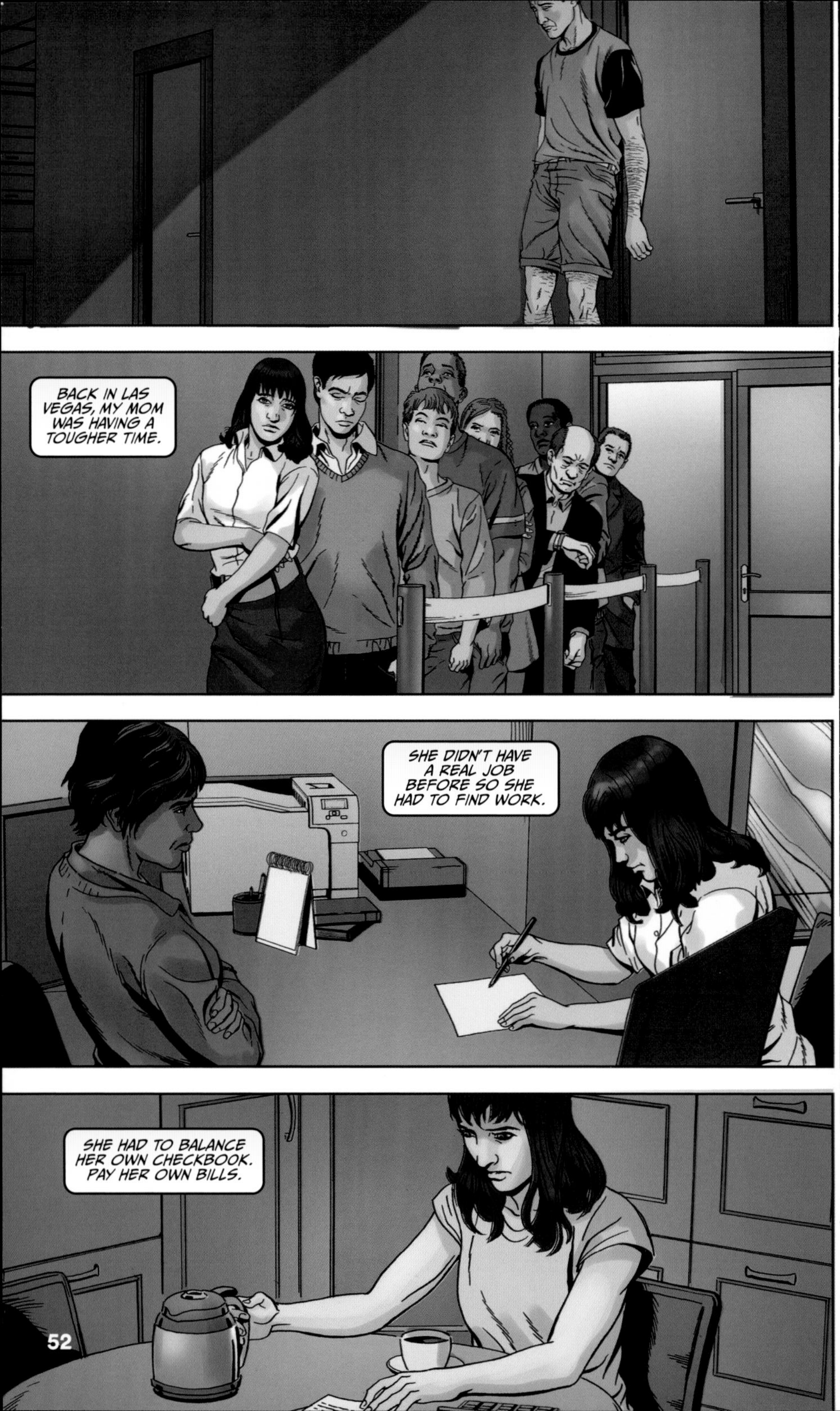
BACK IN LAS VEGAS, MY MOM WAS HAVING A TOUGHER TIME.
SHE DIDN'T HAVE A REAL JOB BEFORE SO SHE HAD TO FIND WORK.
SHE HAD TO BALANCE HER OWN CHECKBOOK. PAY HER OWN BILLS.

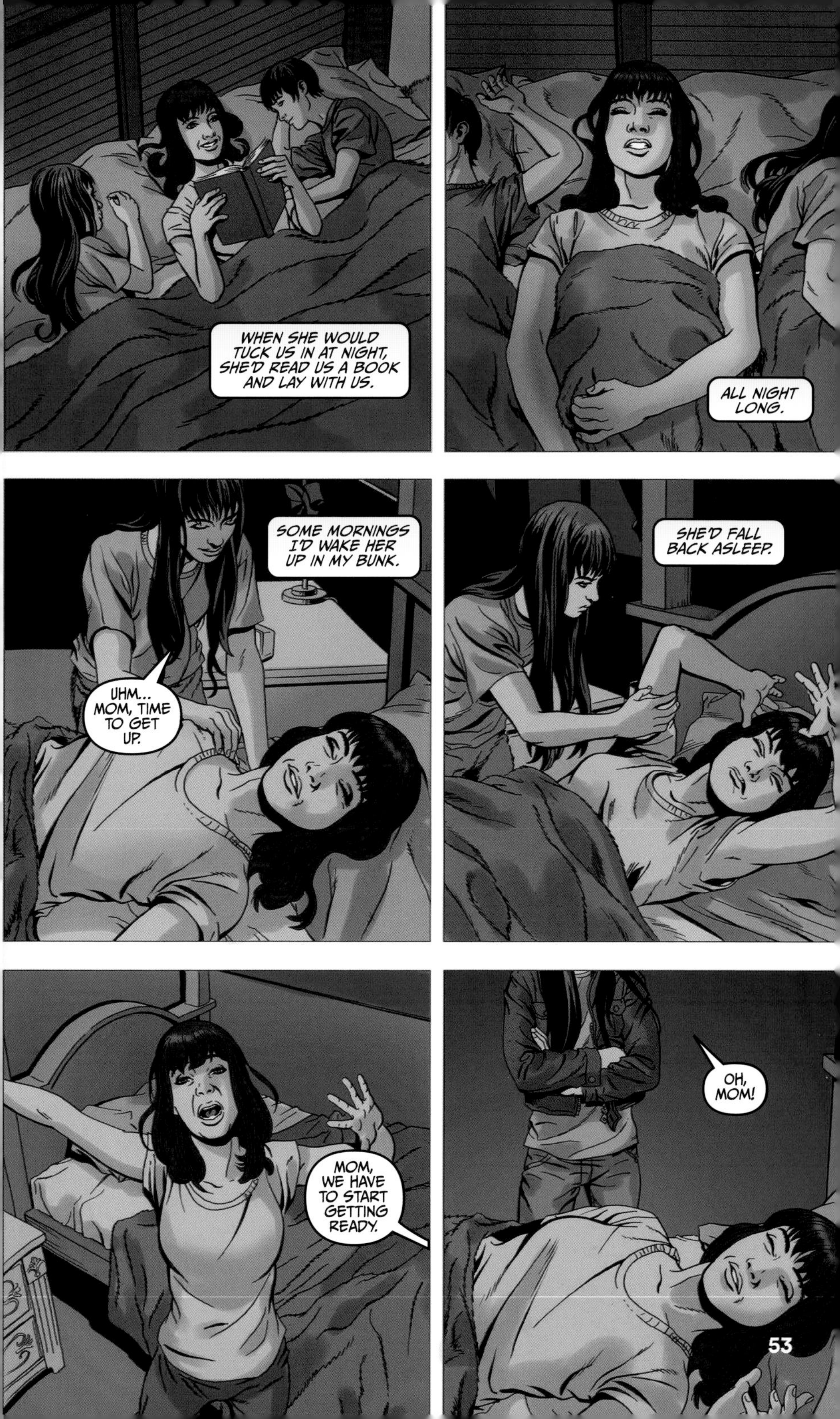
WHEN SHE WOULD TUCK US IN AT NIGHT, SHE'D READ US A BOOK AND LAY WITH US.
ALL NIGHT LONG.
SOME MORNINGS I'D WAKE HER UP IN MY BUNK.
UHM... MOM, TIME TO GET UP.
SHE'D FALL BACK ASLEEP.
MOM, WE HAVE TO START GETTING READY.
OH, MOM!

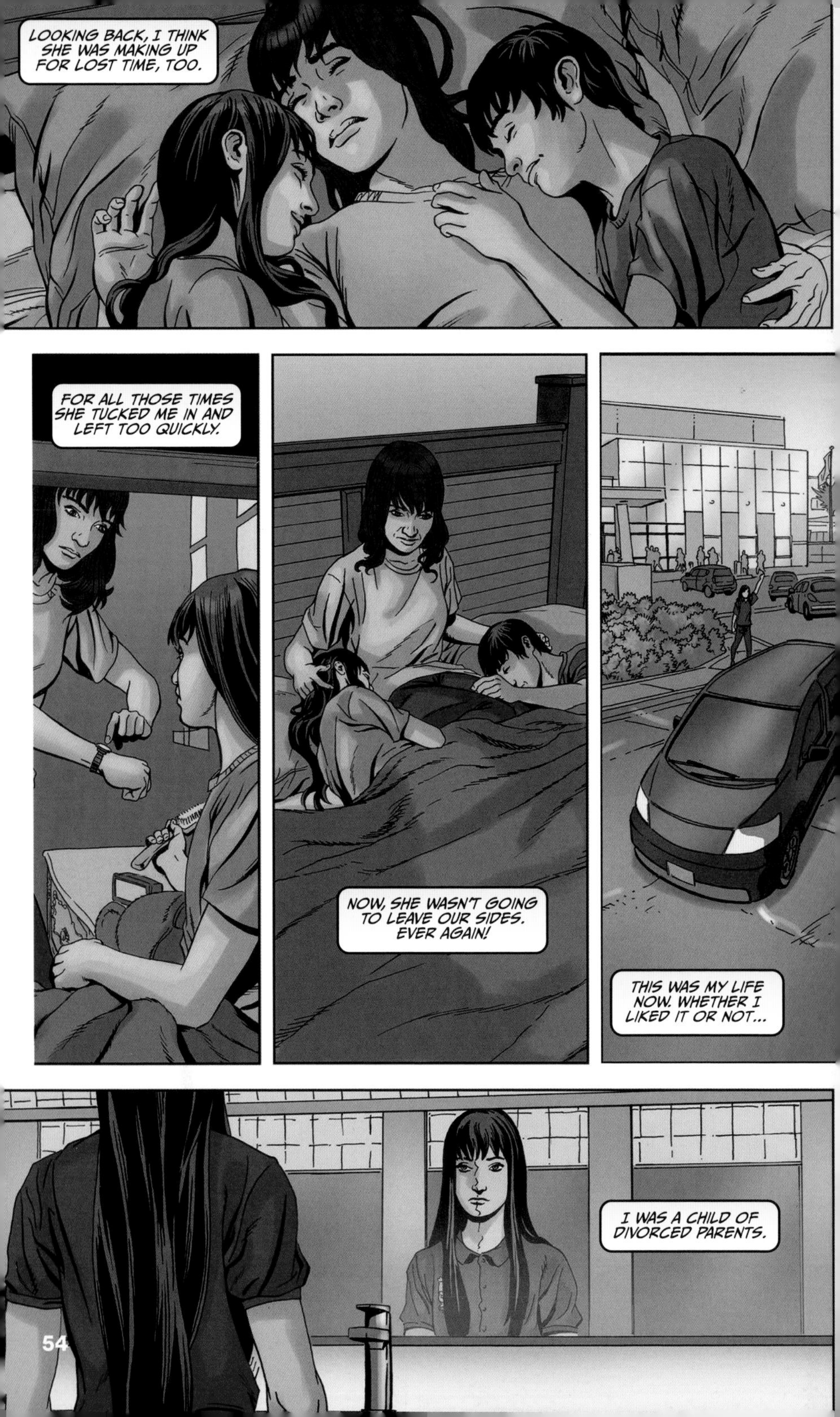
LOOKING BACK, I THINK SHE WAS MAKING UP FOR LOST TIME, TOO.
FOR ALL THOSE TIMES SHE TUCKED ME IN AND LEFT TOO QUICKLY.
NOW, SHE WASN'T GOING TO LEAVE OUR SIDES. EVER AGAIN!
THIS WAS MY LIFE NOW. WHETHER I LIKED IT OR NOT...
I WAS A CHILD OF DIVORCED PARENTS.

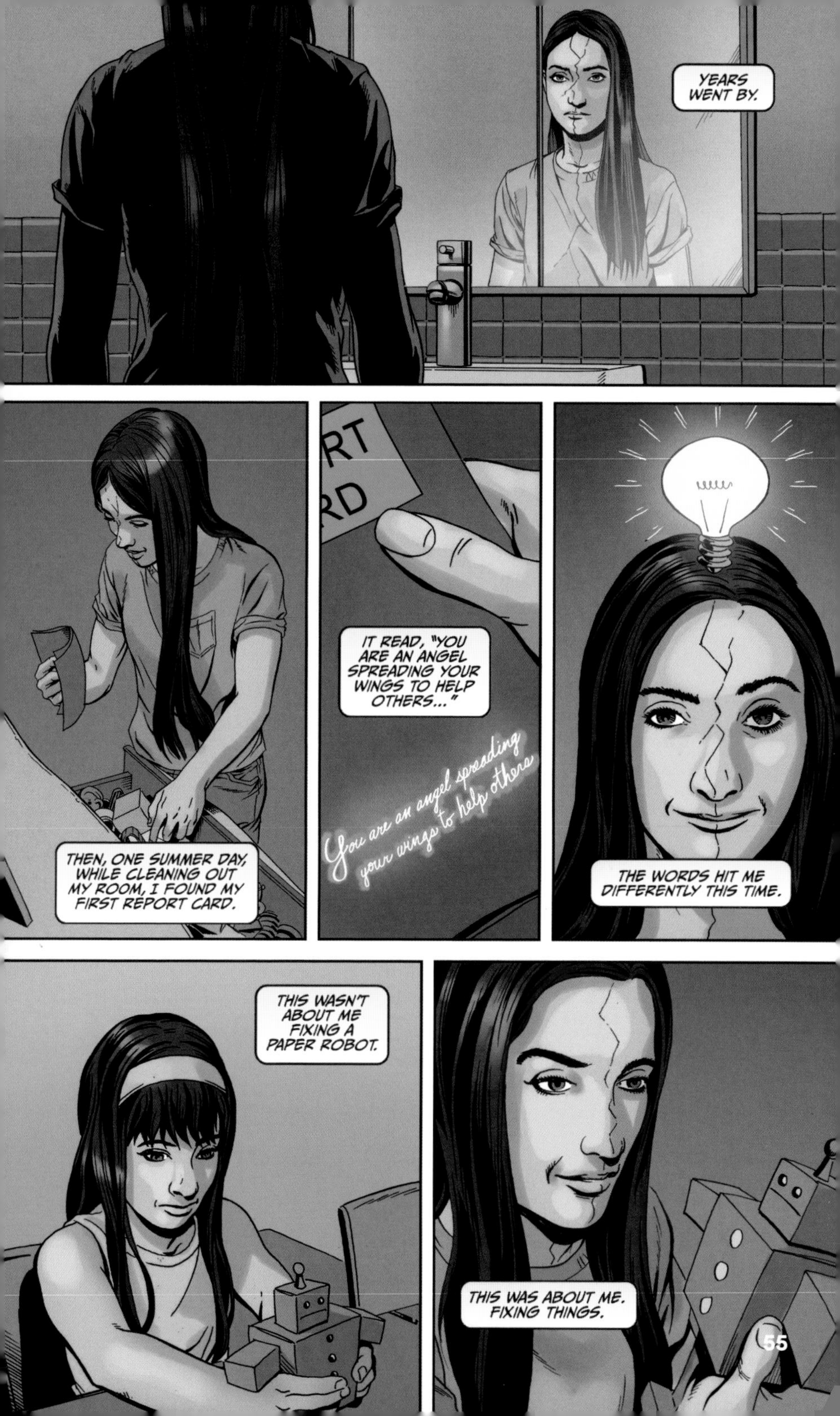

YEARS WENT BY.
THEN, ONE SUMMER DAY, WHILE CLEANING OUT MY ROOM, I FOUND MY FIRST REPORT CARD.
IT READ, "YOU ARE AN ANGEL SPREADING YOUR WINGS TO HELP OTHERS..."
You are an angel spreading your wings to help others
THE WORDS HIT ME DIFFERENTLY THIS TIME.
THIS WASN'T ABOUT ME FIXING A PAPER ROBOT.
THIS WAS ABOUT ME. FIXING THINGS.

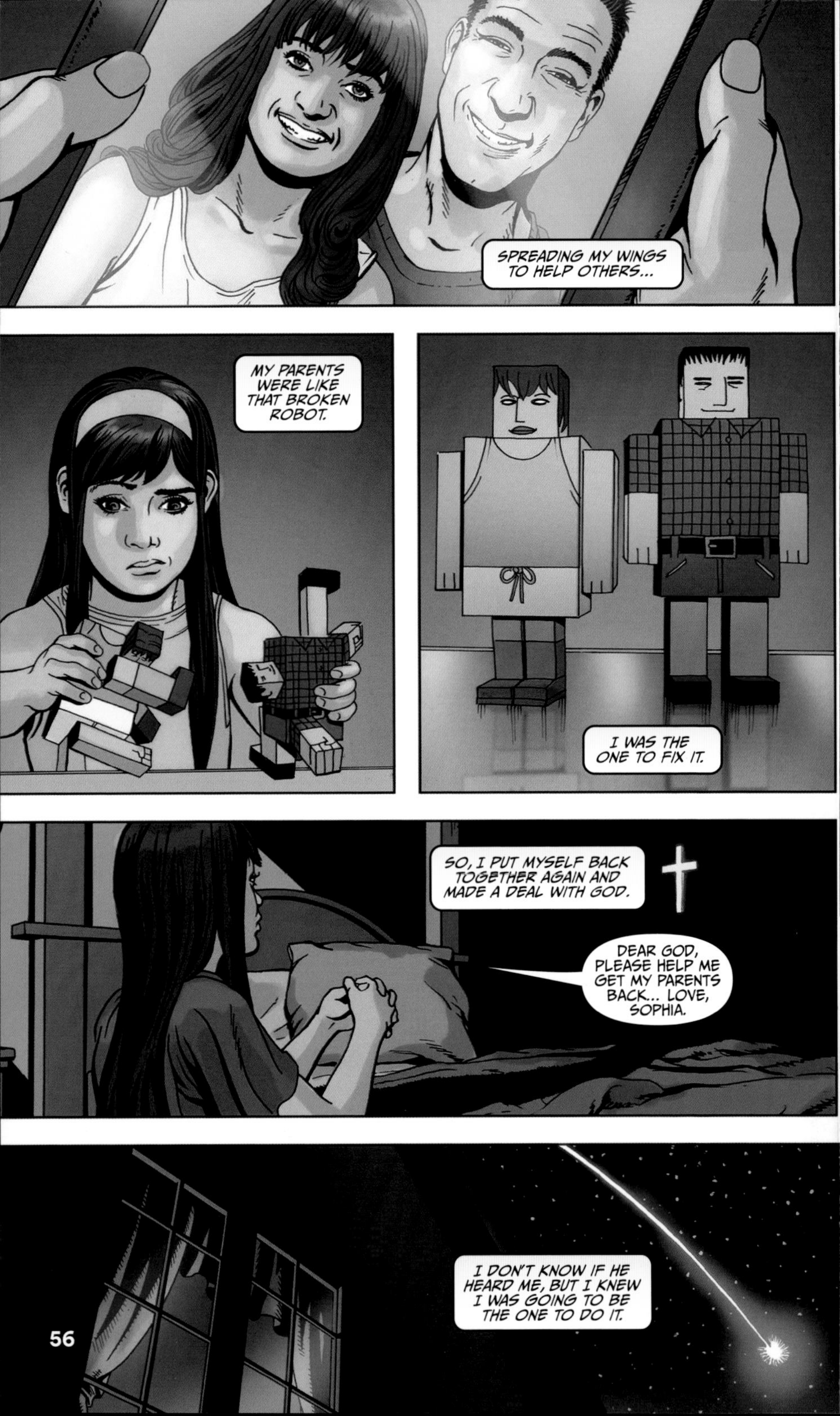
SPREADING MY WINGS TO HELP OTHERS...
MY PARENTS WERE LIKE THAT BROKEN ROBOT.
I WAS THE ONE TO FIX IT.
SO, I PUT MYSELF BACK TOGETHER AGAIN AND MADE A DEAL WITH GOD.
DEAR GOD, PLEASE HELP ME GET MY PARENTS BACK... LOVE, SOPHIA.
I DON'T KNOW IF HE HEARD ME, BUT I KNEW I WAS GOING TO BE THE ONE TO DO IT.

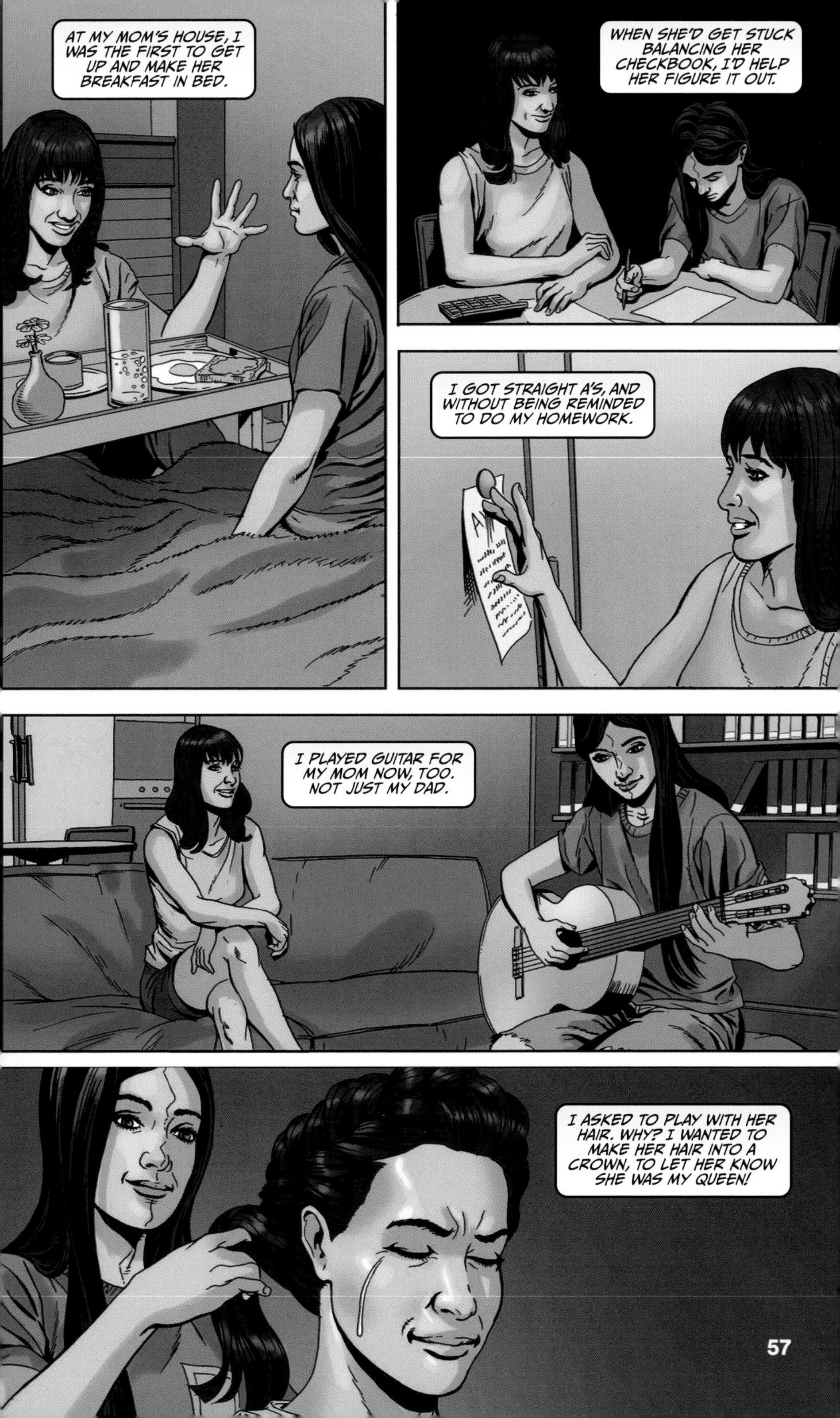
AT MY MOM'S HOUSE, I WAS THE FIRST TO GET UP AND MAKE HER BREAKFAST IN BED.
WHEN SHE'D GET STUCK BALANCING HER CHECKBOOK, I'D HELP HER FIGURE IT OUT.
I GOT STRAIGHT A'S, AND WITHOUT BEING REMINDED TO DO MY HOMEWORK.
I PLAYED GUITAR FOR MY MOM NOW, TOO. NOT JUST MY DAD.
I ASKED TO PLAY WITH HER HAIR. WHY? I WANTED TO MAKE HER HAIR INTO A CROWN, TO LET HER KNOW SHE WAS MY QUEEN!

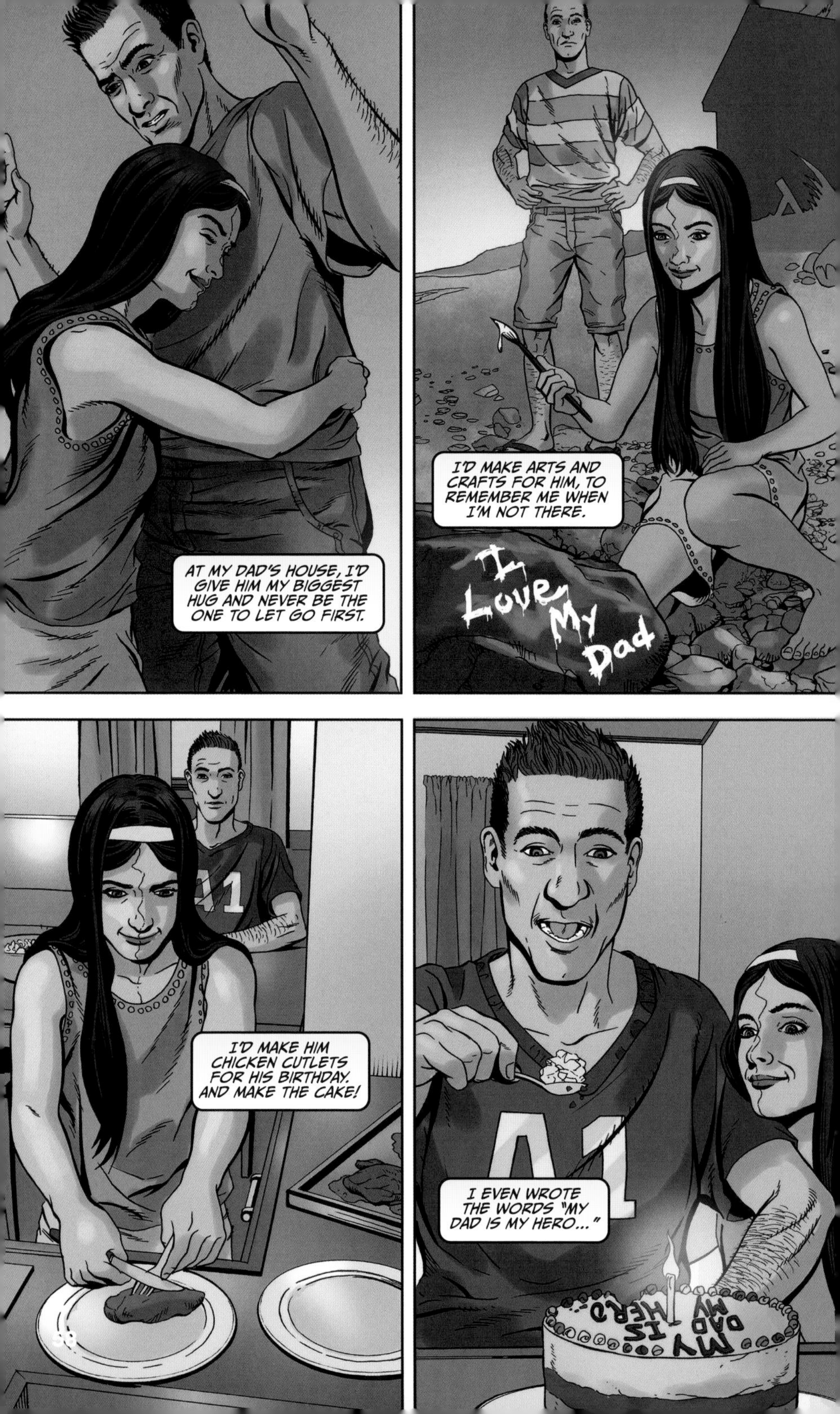
AT MY DAD'S HOUSE, I'D GIVE HIM MY BIGGEST HUG AND NEVER BE THE ONE TO LET GO FIRST.
I'D MAKE ARTS AND CRAFTS FOR HIM, TO REMEMBER ME WHEN I'M NOT THERE.
I Love My Dad
I'D MAKE HIM CHICKEN CUTLETS FOR HIS BIRTHDAY. AND MAKE THE CAKE!
I EVEN WROTE THE WORDS "MY DAD IS MY HERO..."
MY DAD IS MY HERO

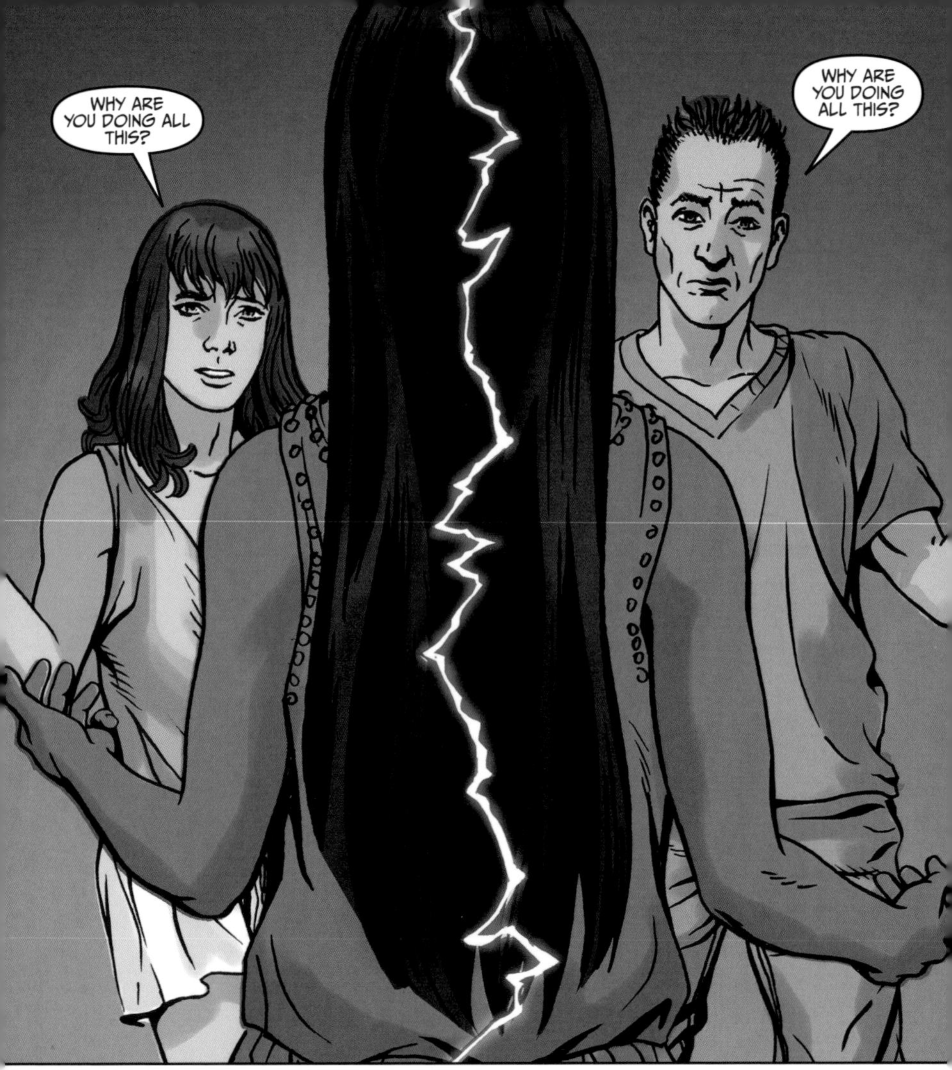
WHY ARE YOU DOING ALL THIS?
WHY ARE YOU DOING ALL THIS?

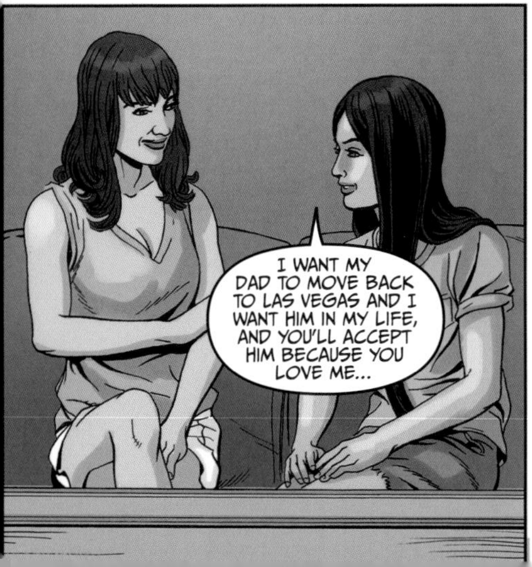
I WANT MY DAD TO MOVE BACK TO LAS VEGAS AND I WANT HIM IN MY LIFE, AND YOU'LL ACCEPT HIM BECAUSE YOU LOVE ME...

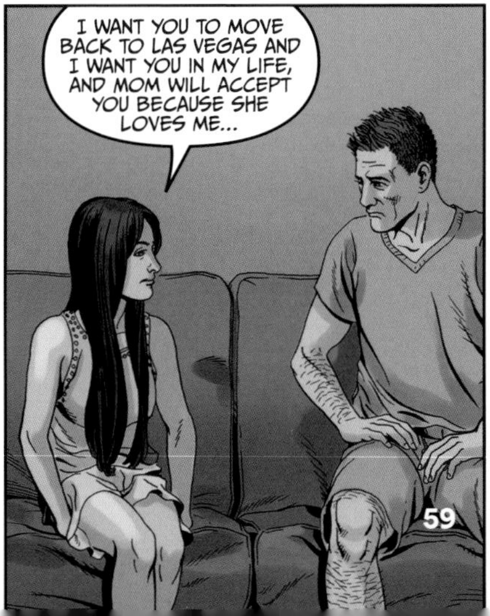
I WANT YOU TO MOVE BACK TO LAS VEGAS AND I WANT YOU IN MY LIFE, AND MOM WILL ACCEPT YOU BECAUSE SHE LOVES ME...

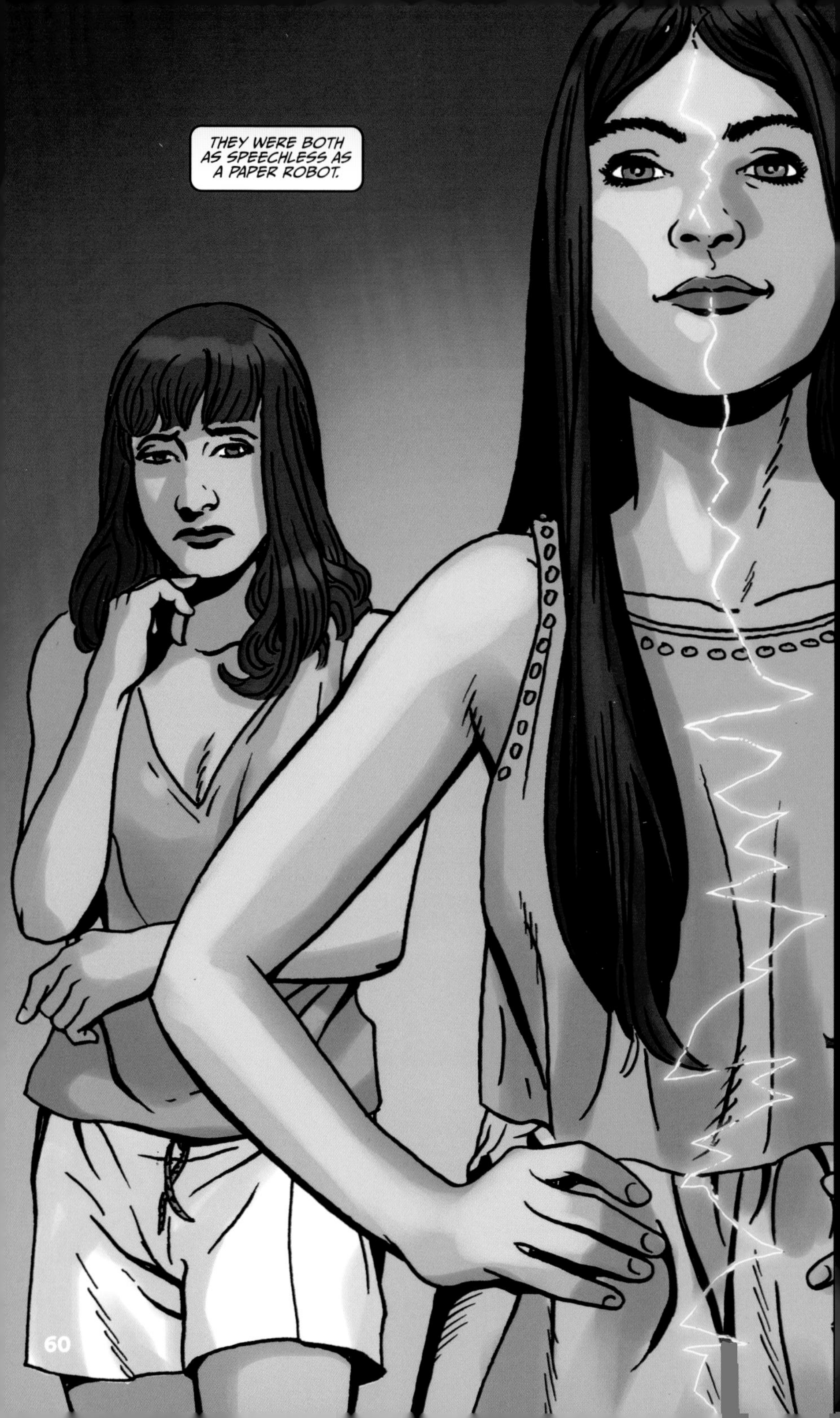
THEY WERE BOTH AS SPEECHLESS AS A PAPER ROBOT.

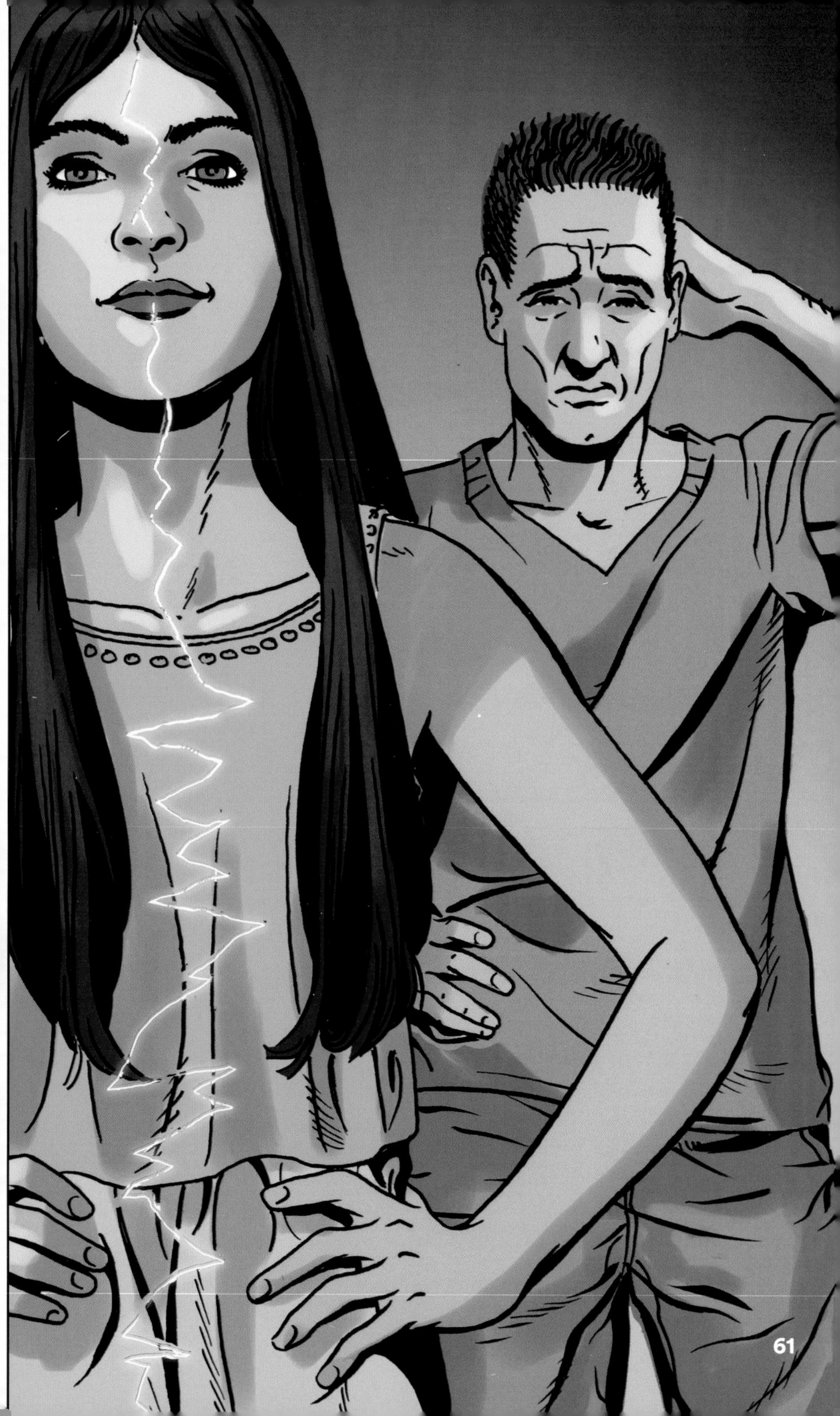

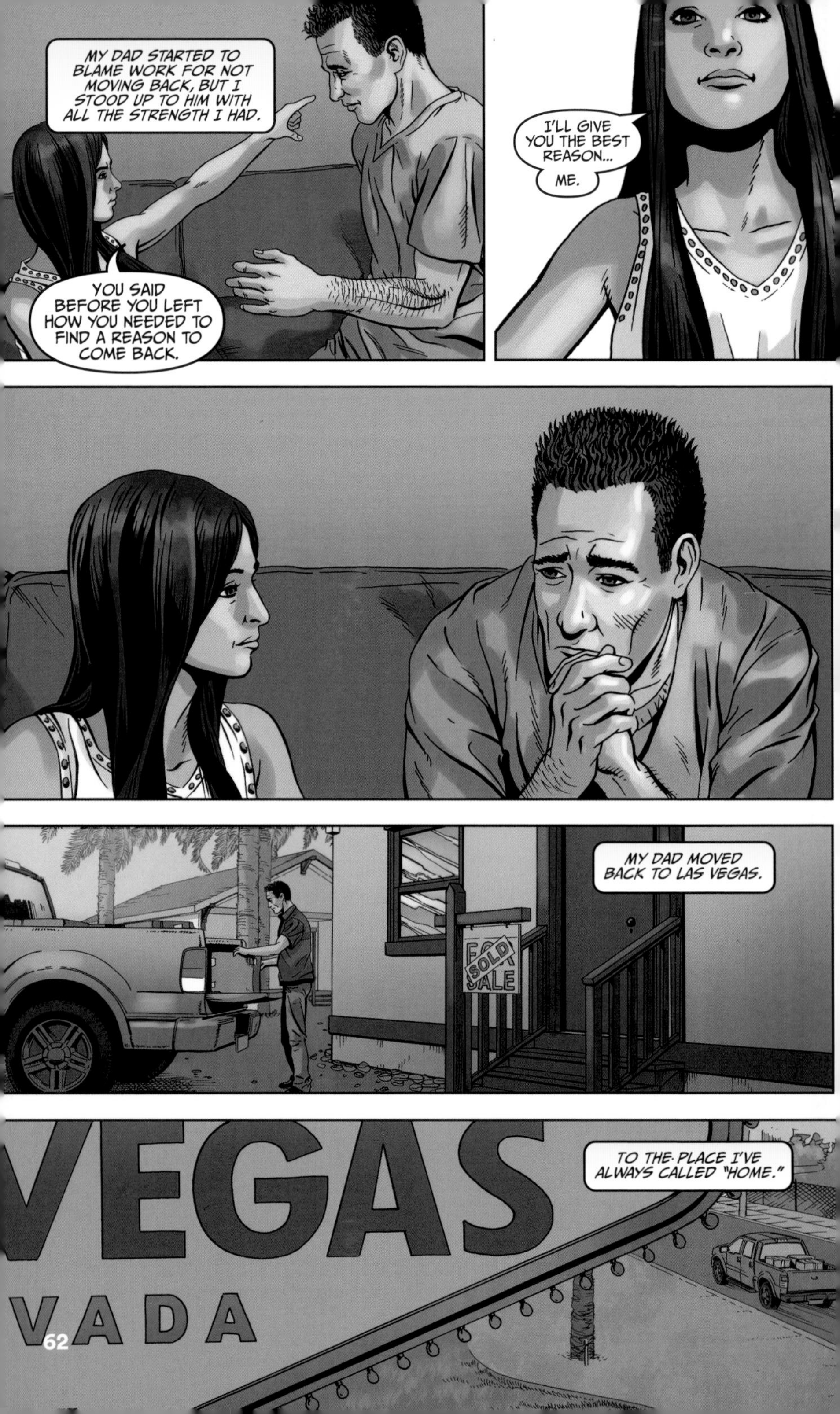
MY DAD STARTED TO BLAME WORK FOR NOT MOVING BACK, BUT I STOOD UP TO HIM WITH ALL THE STRENGTH I HAD.
YOU SAID BEFORE YOU LEFT HOW YOU NEEDED TO FIND A REASON TO COME BACK.
I'LL GIVE YOU THE BEST REASON...
ME.
MY DAD MOVED BACK TO LAS VEGAS.
SOLD
TO THE PLACE I'VE ALWAYS CALLED "HOME."
VEGAS
VADA

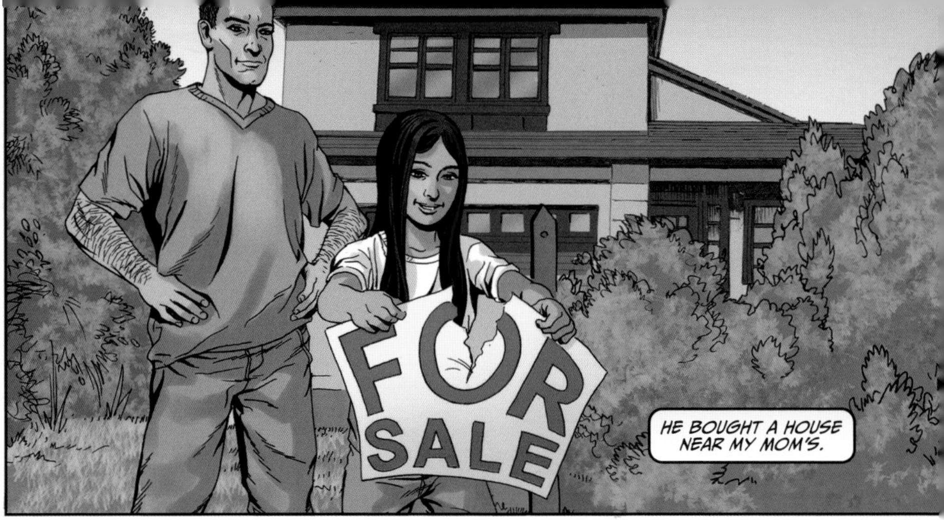
FOR SALE
HE BOUGHT A HOUSE NEAR MY MOM'S.

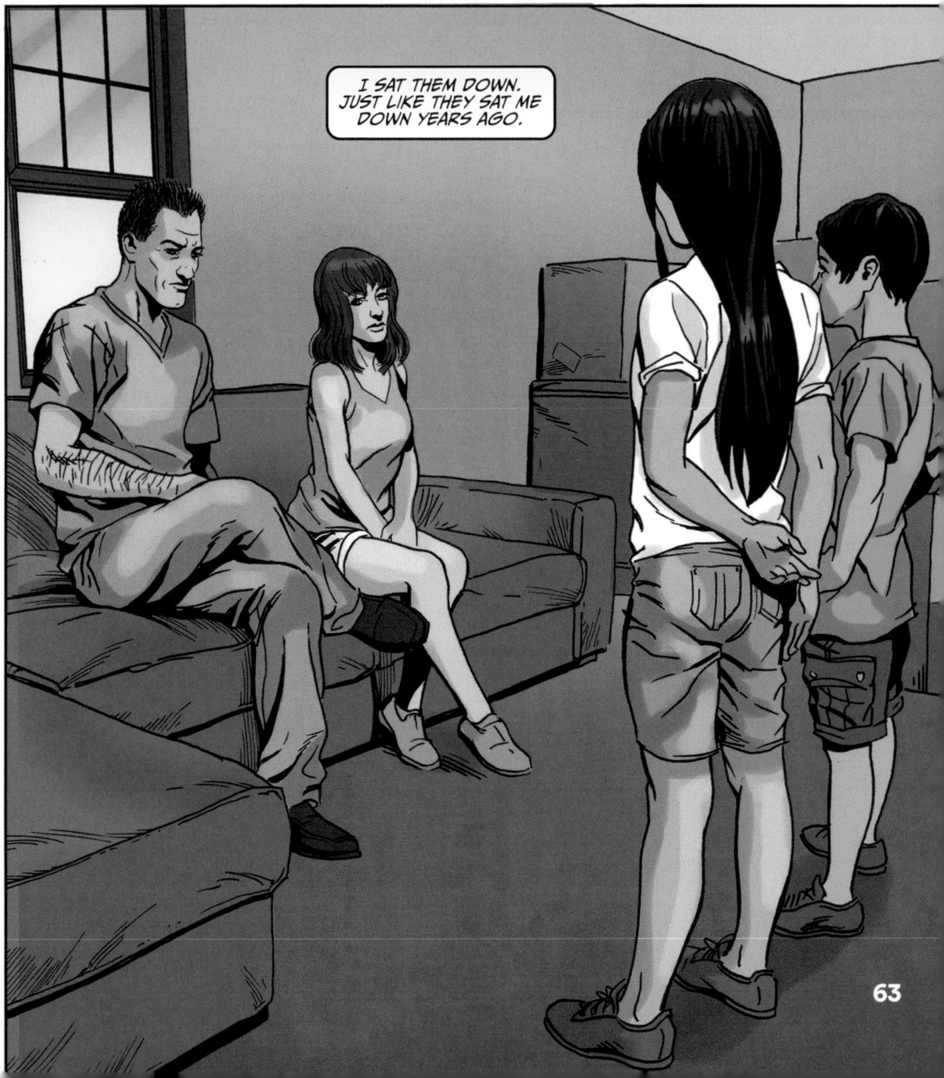
I SAT THEM DOWN. JUST LIKE THEY SAT ME DOWN YEARS AGO.

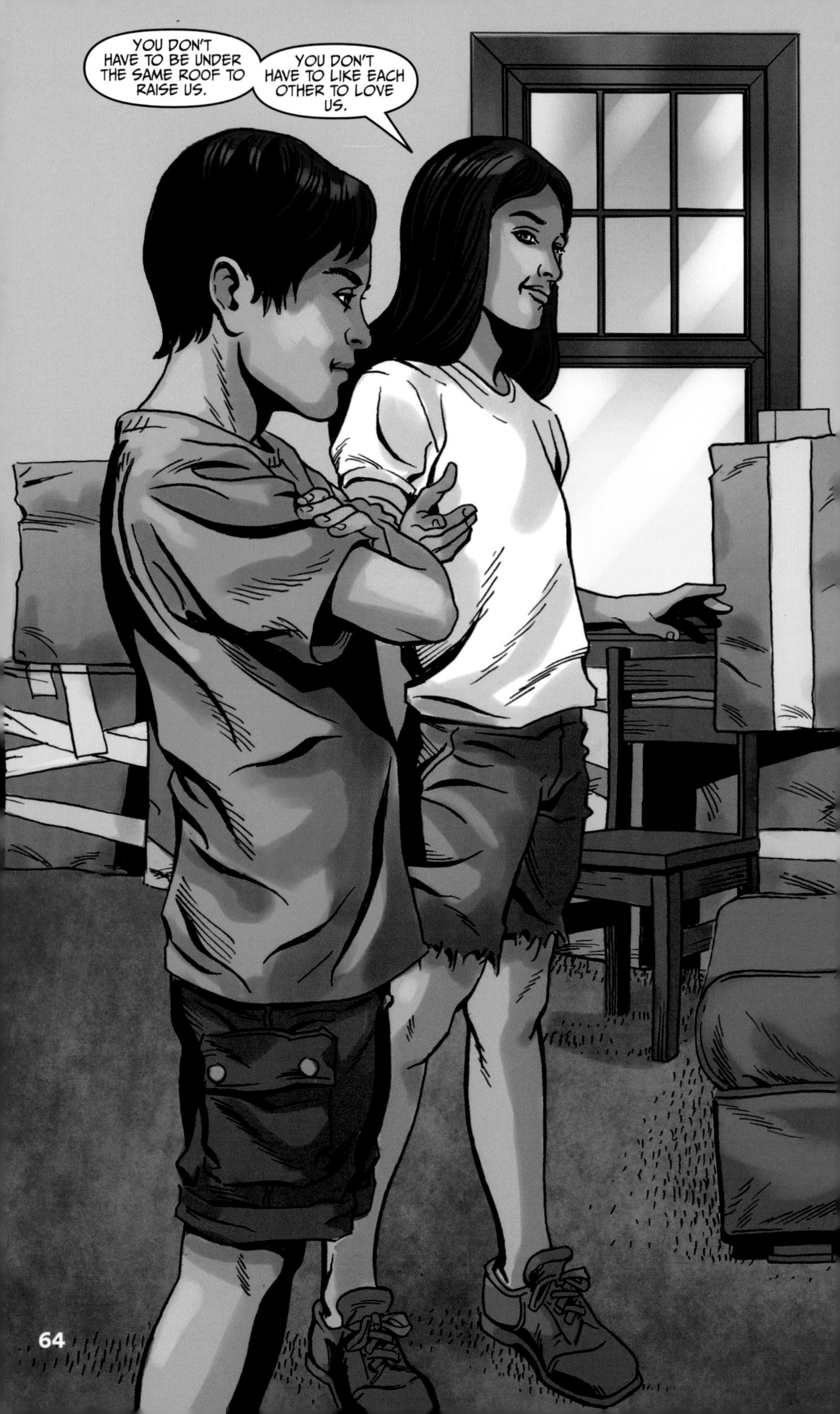
YOU DON'T HAVE TO BE UNDER THE SAME ROOF TO RAISE US.
YOU DON'T HAVE TO LIKE EACH OTHER TO LOVE US.

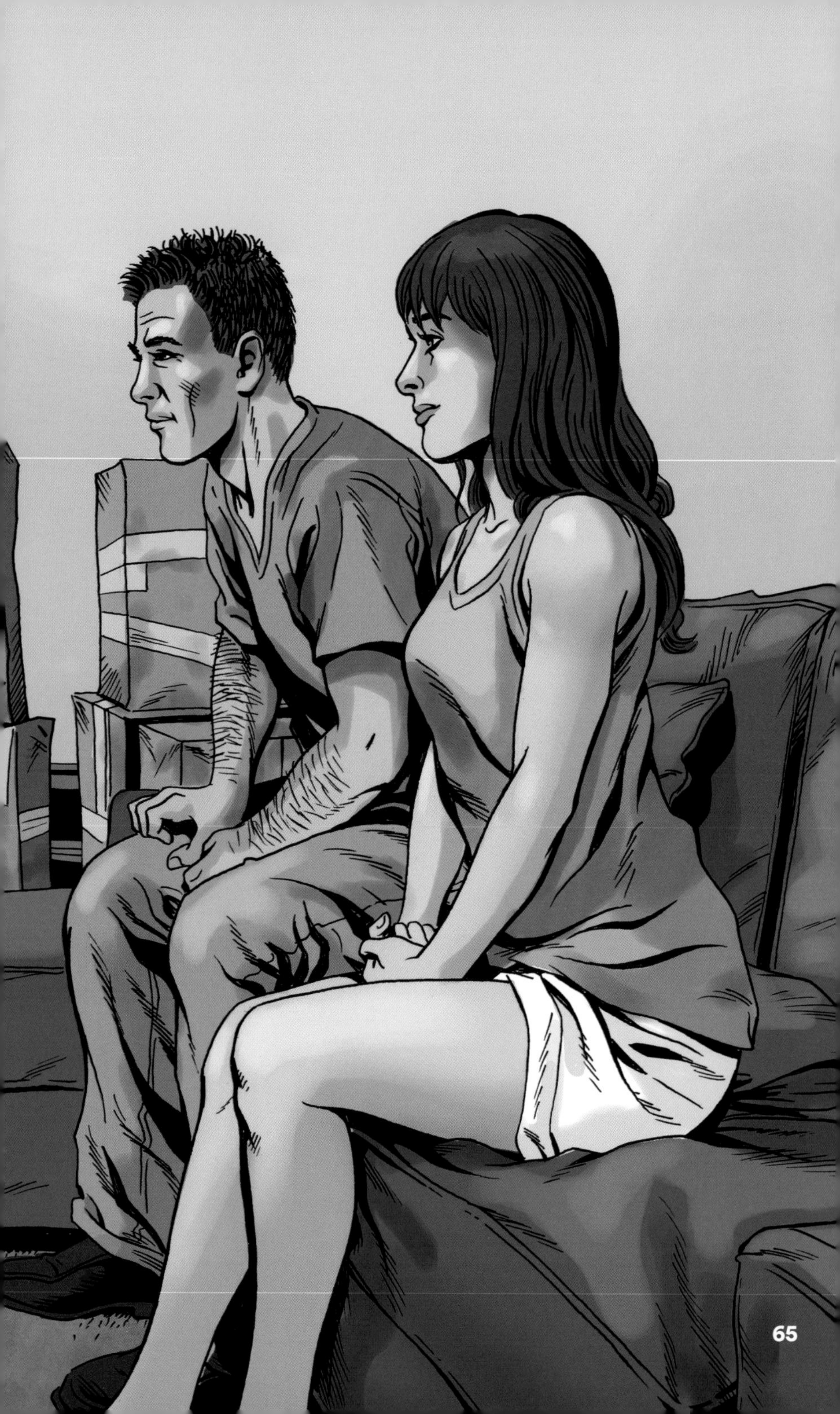

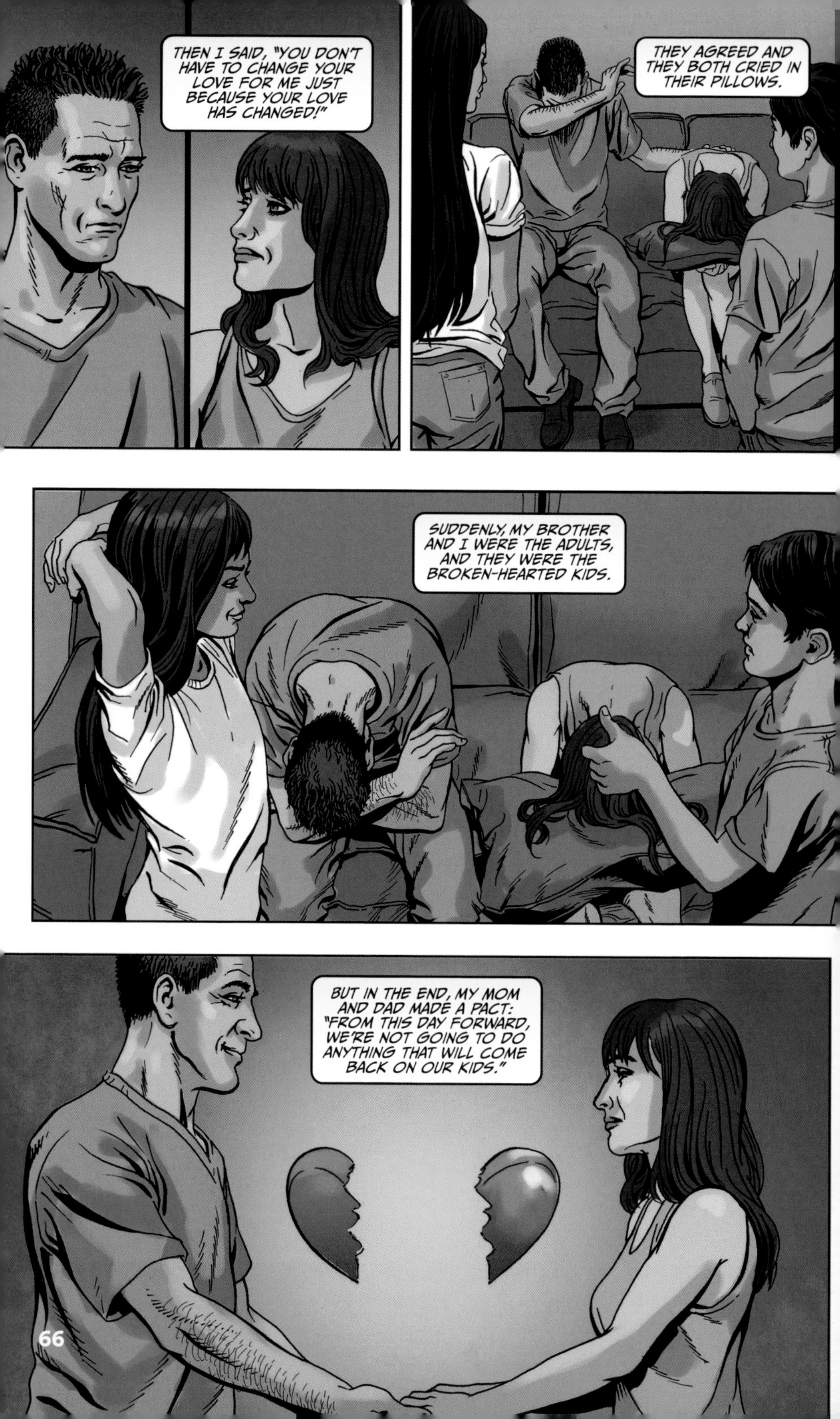

THEN I SAID, "YOU DON'T HAVE TO CHANGE YOUR LOVE FOR ME JUST BECAUSE YOUR LOVE HAS CHANGED!"
THEY AGREED AND THEY BOTH CRIED IN THEIR PILLOWS.
SUDDENLY, MY BROTHER AND I WERE THE ADULTS, AND THEY WERE THE BROKEN-HEARTED KIDS.
BUT IN THE END, MY MOM AND DAD MADE A PACT: "FROM THIS DAY FORWARD, WE'RE NOT GOING TO DO ANYTHING THAT WILL COME BACK ON OUR KIDS."

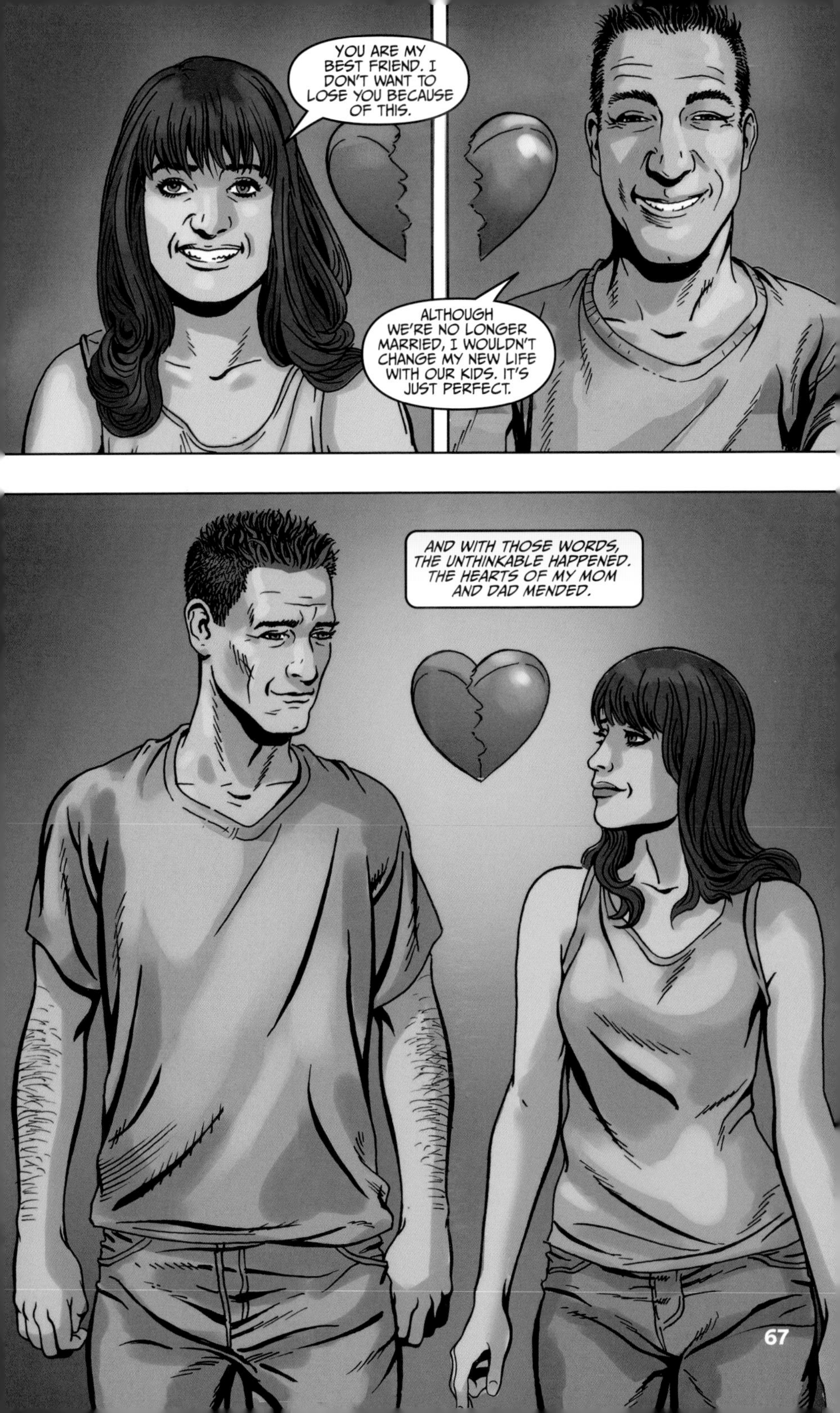
YOU ARE MY BEST FRIEND. I DON'T WANT TO LOSE YOU BECAUSE OF THIS.
ALTHOUGH WE'RE NO LONGER MARRIED, I WOULDN'T CHANGE MY NEW LIFE WITH OUR KIDS. IT'S JUST PERFECT.
AND WITH THOSE WORDS, THE UNTHINKABLE HAPPENED. THE HEARTS OF MY MOM AND DAD MENDED.

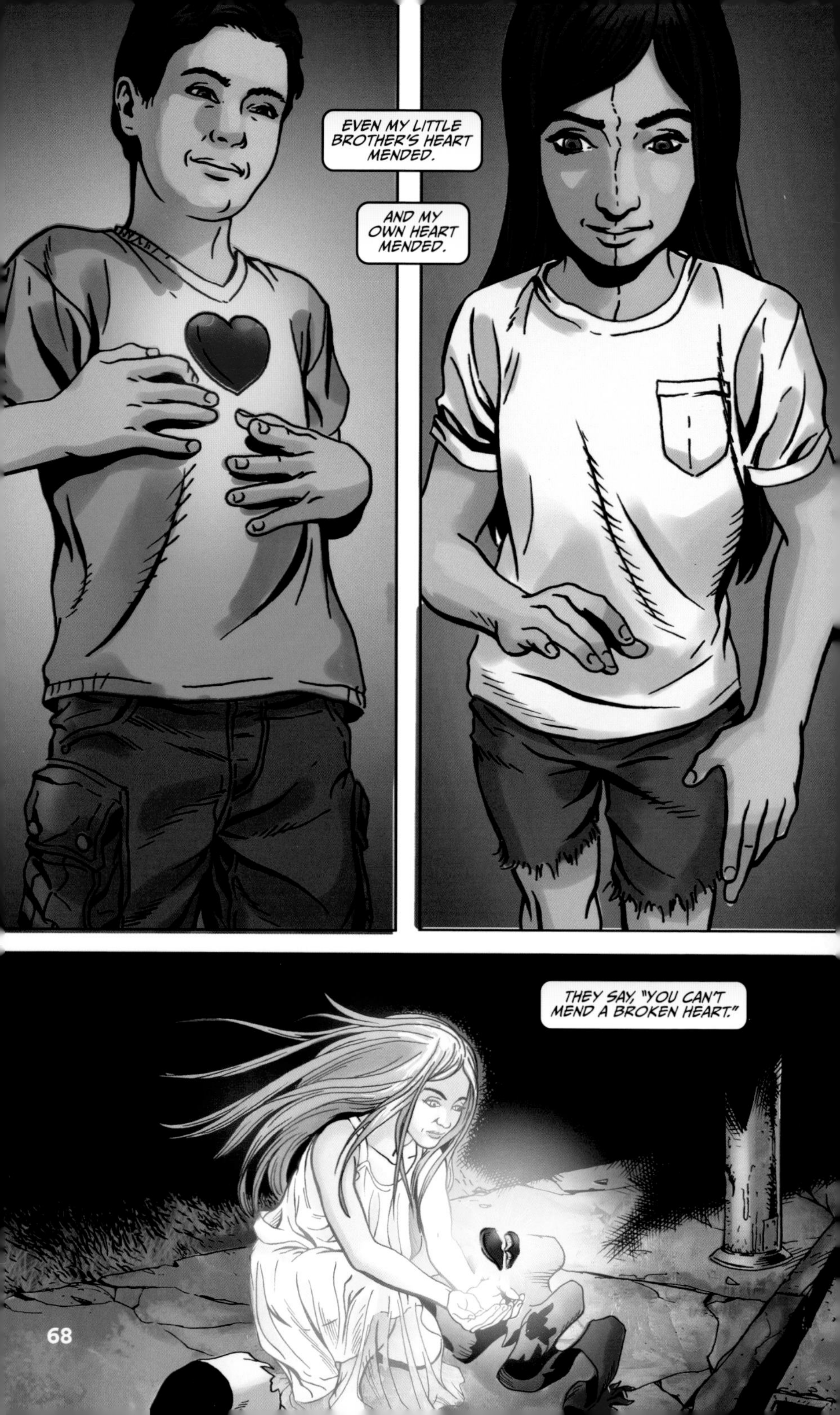
EVEN MY LITTLE BROTHER'S HEART MENDED.
AND MY OWN HEART MENDED.
THEY SAY, "YOU CAN'T MEND A BROKEN HEART."

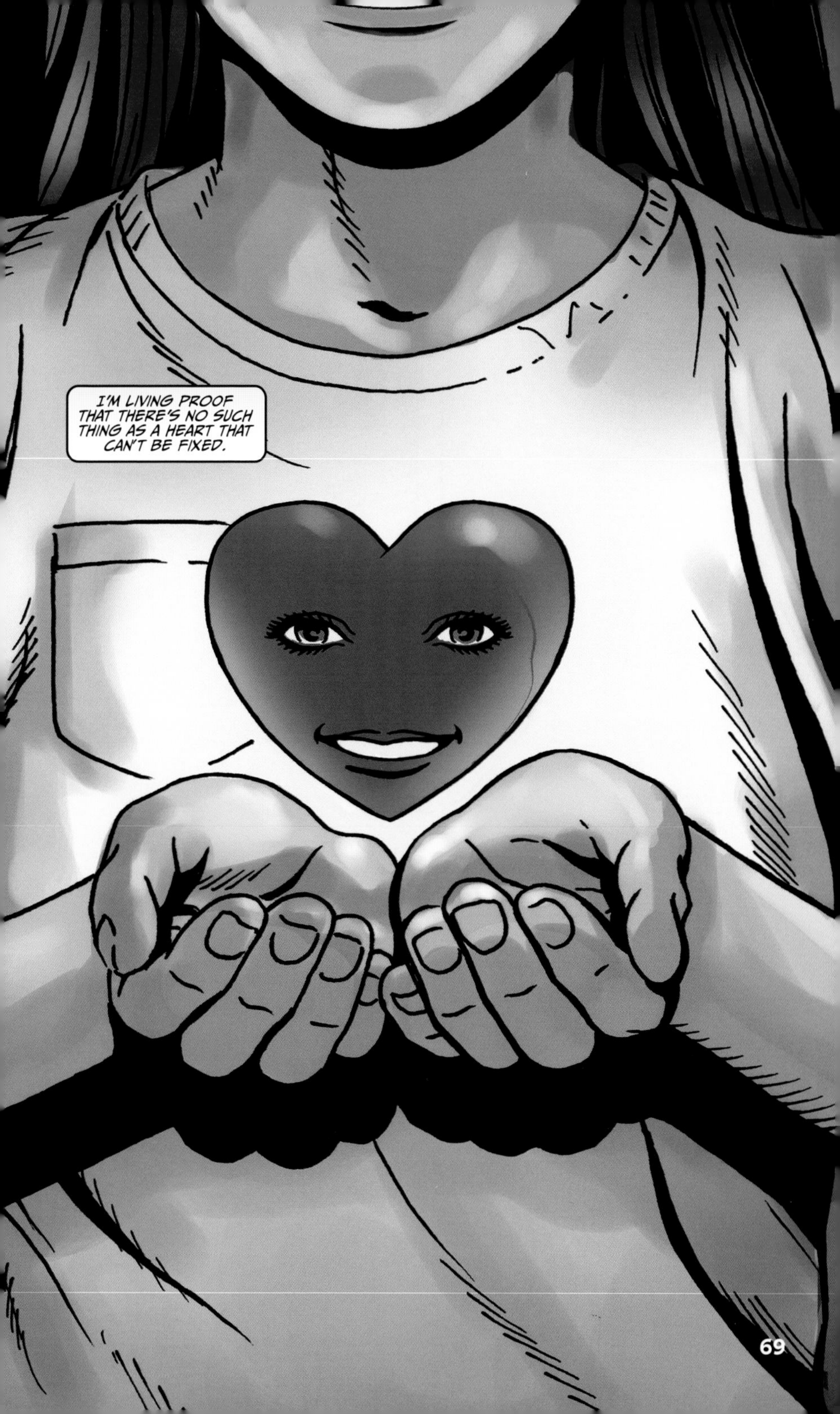
I'M LIVING PROOF THAT THERE'S NO SUCH THING AS A HEART THAT CAN'T BE FIXED.

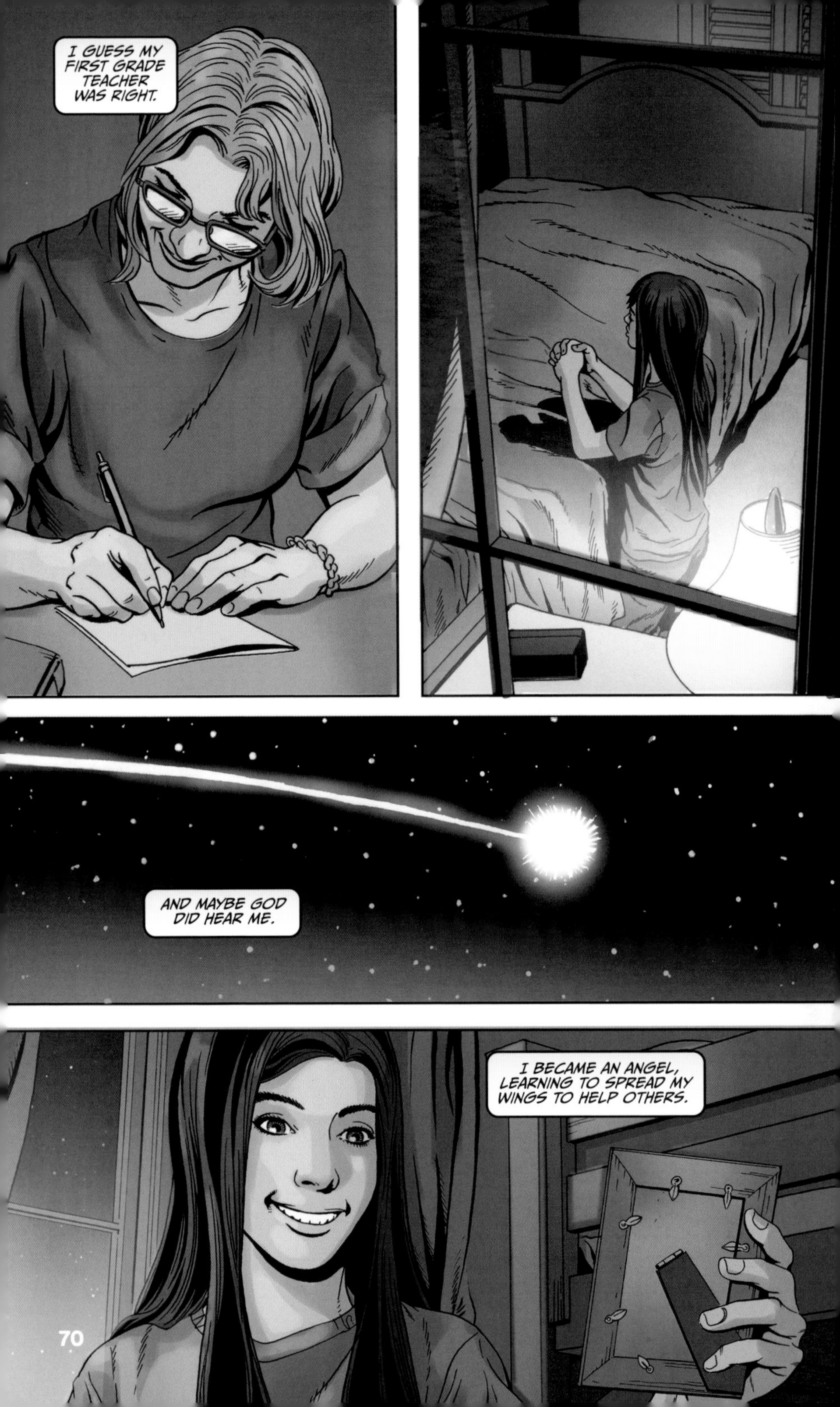
I GUESS MY FIRST GRADE TEACHER WAS RIGHT.
AND MAYBE GOD DID HEAR ME.
I BECAME AN ANGEL, LEARNING TO SPREAD MY WINGS TO HELP OTHERS.

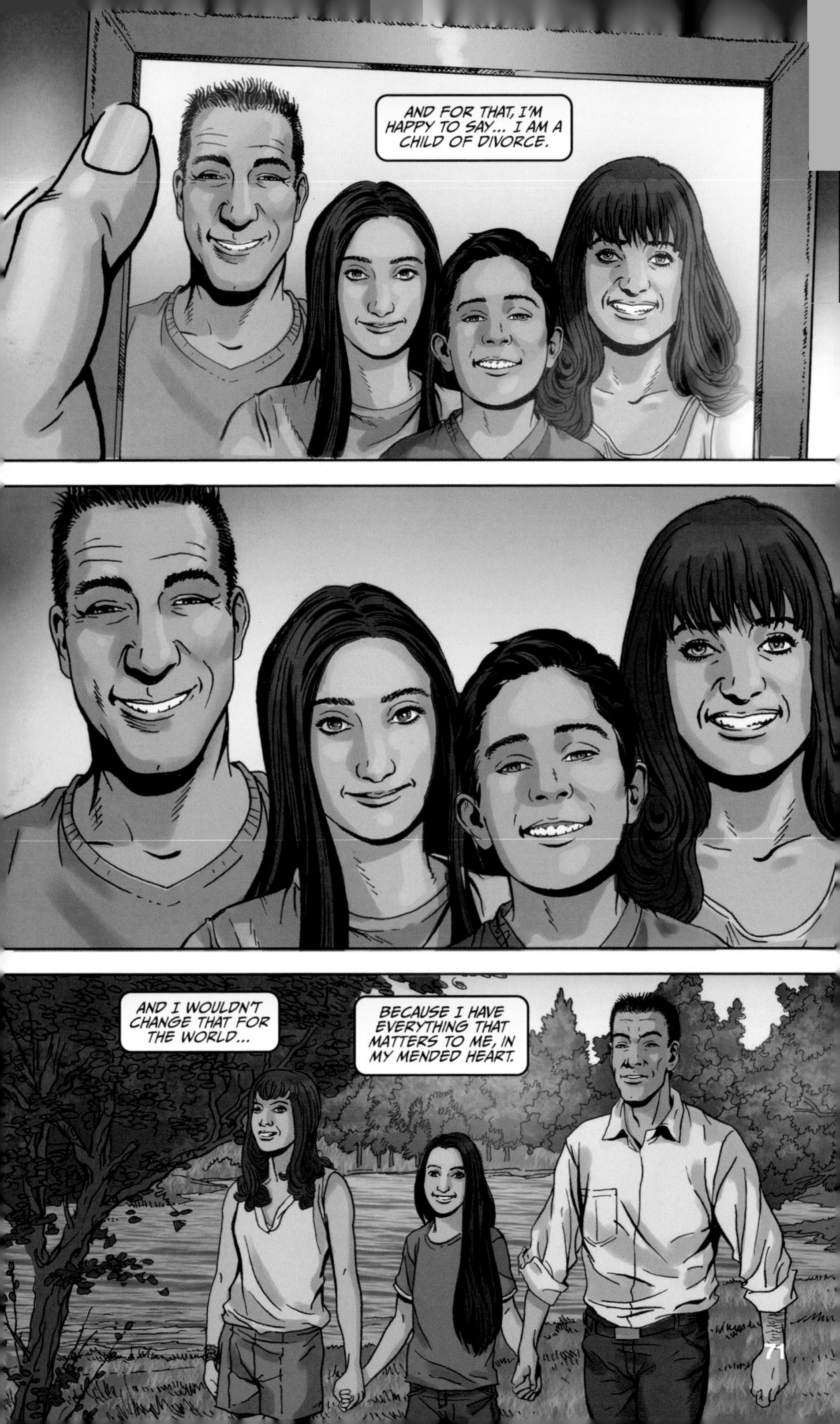
AND FOR THAT, I'M HAPPY TO SAY... I AM A CHILD OF DIVORCE.
AND I WOULDN'T CHANGE THAT FOR THE WORLD...
BECAUSE I HAVE EVERYTHING THAT MATTERS TO ME, IN MY MENDED HEART.

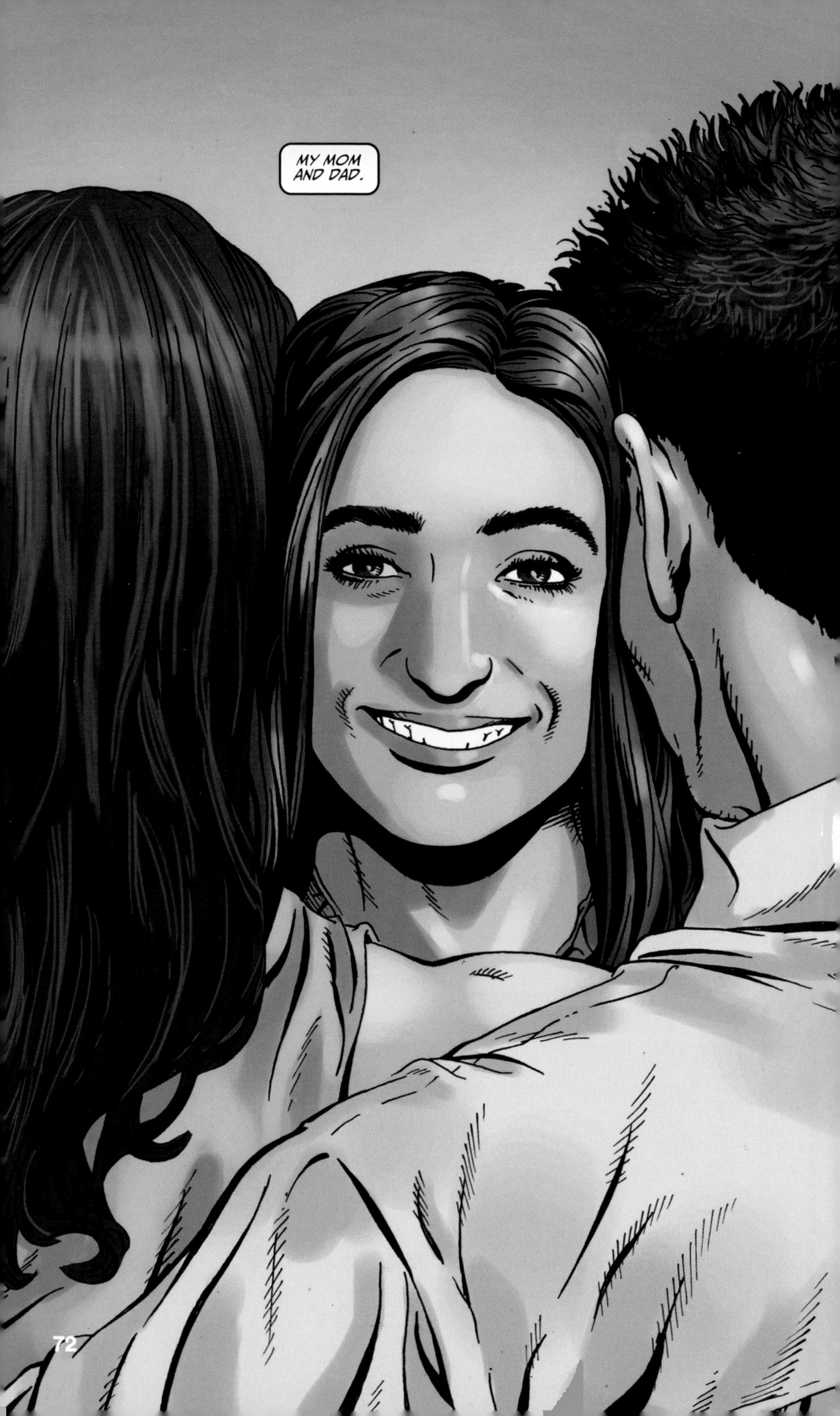
MY MOM AND DAD.

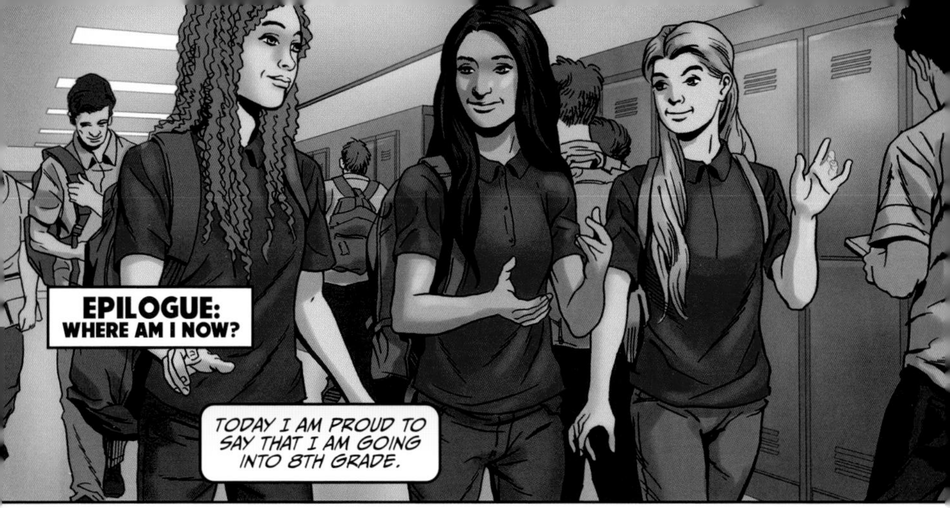
EPILOGUE:
WHERE AM I NOW?
TODAY I AM PROUD TO SAY THAT I AM GOING INTO 8TH GRADE.

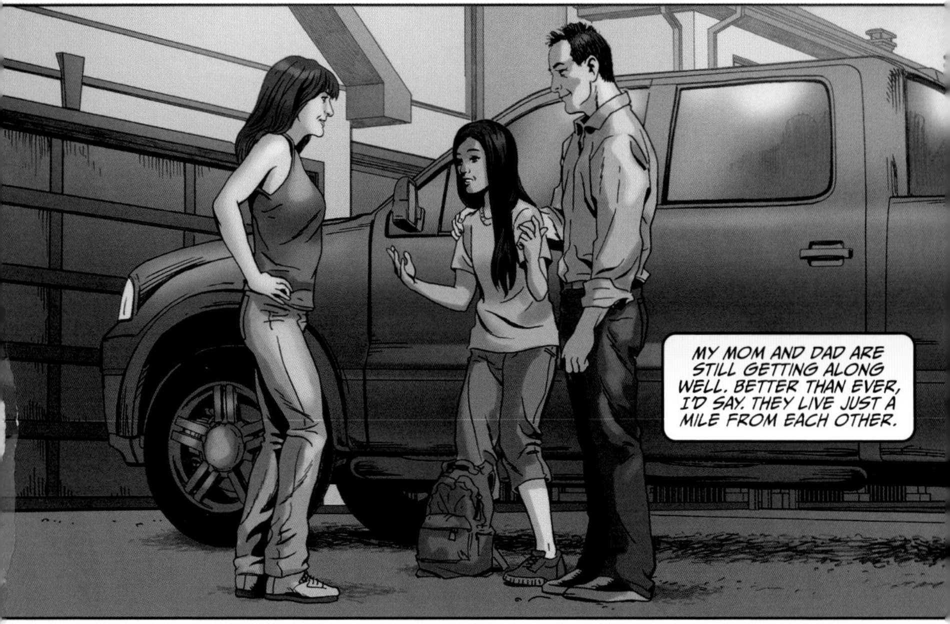
MY MOM AND DAD ARE STILL GETTING ALONG WELL. BETTER THAN EVER, I'D SAY. THEY LIVE JUST A MILE FROM EACH OTHER.

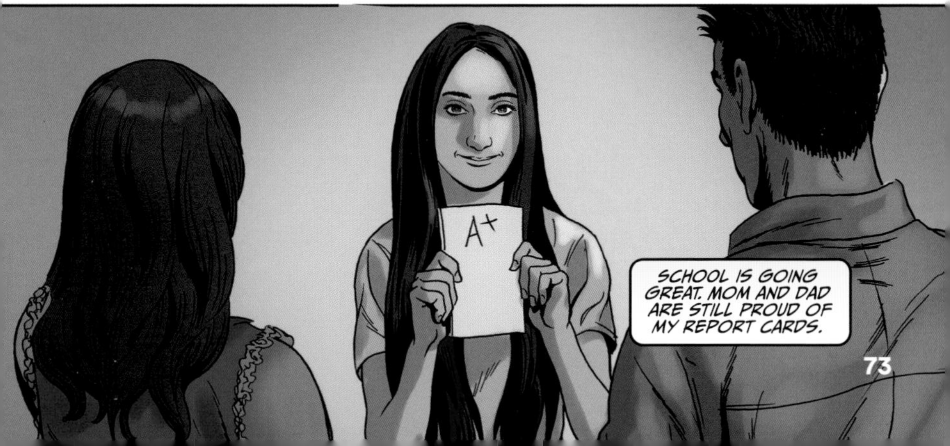
A+
SCHOOL IS GOING GREAT. MOM AND DAD ARE STILL PROUD OF MY REPORT CARDS.

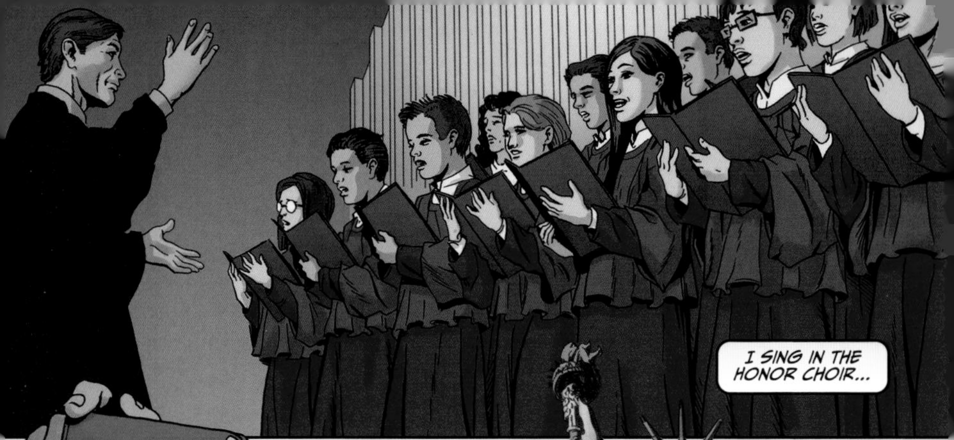
I SING IN THE HONOR CHOIR...

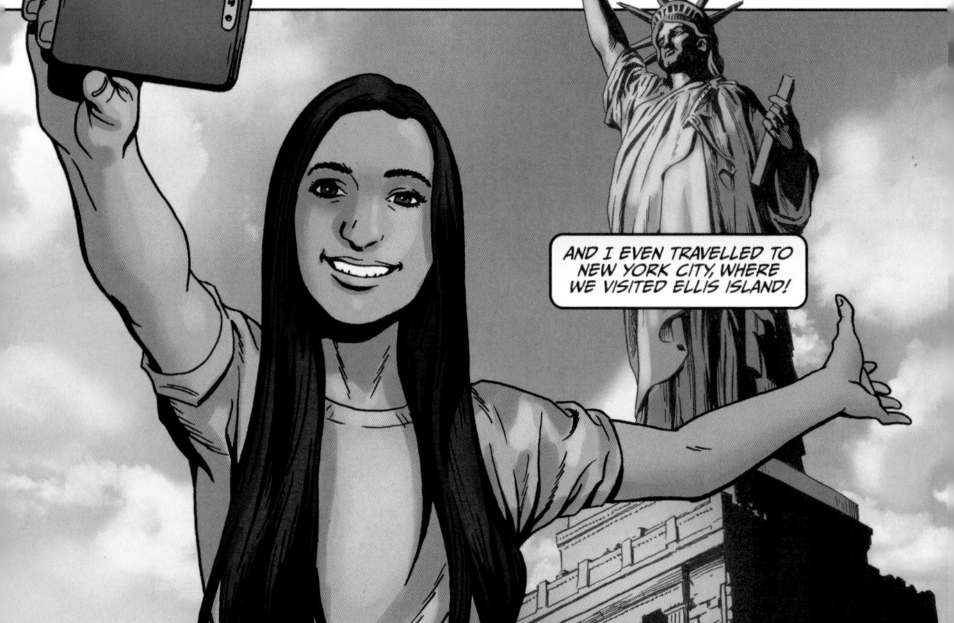
AND I EVEN TRAVELLED TO NEW YORK CITY, WHERE WE VISITED ELLIS ISLAND!

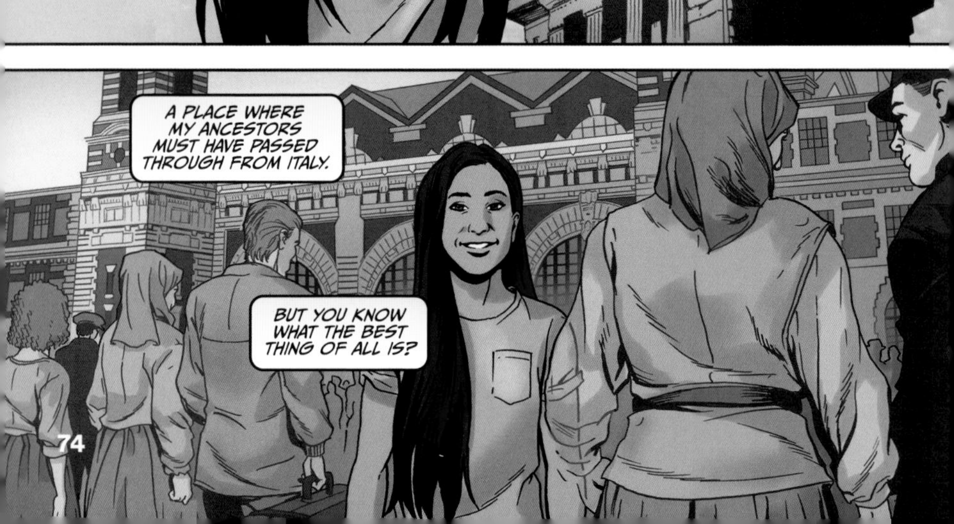
A PLACE WHERE MY ANCESTORS MUST HAVE PASSED THROUGH FROM ITALY.
BUT YOU KNOW WHAT THE BEST THING OF ALL IS?

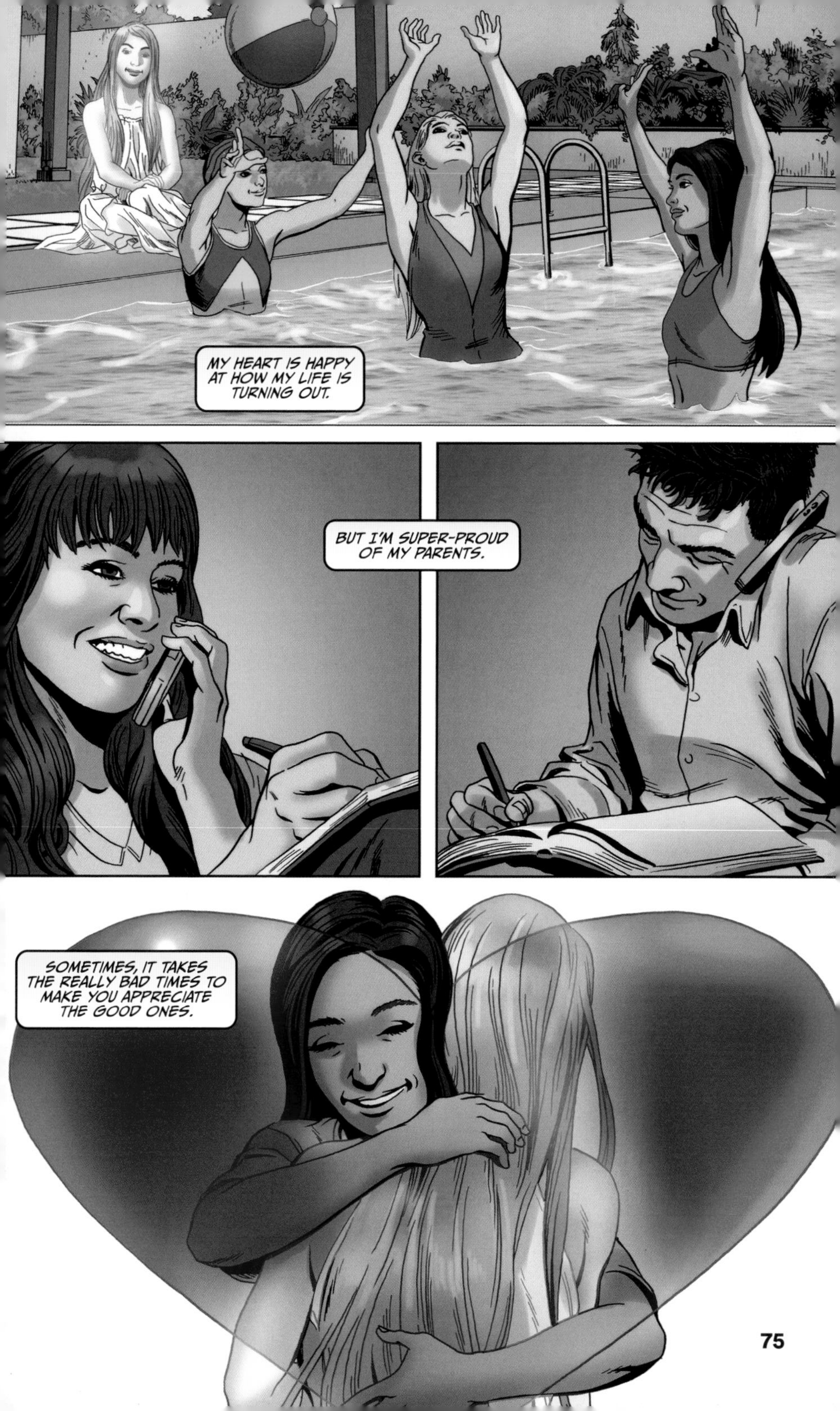
MY HEART IS HAPPY AT HOW MY LIFE IS TURNING OUT.
BUT I'M SUPER-PROUD OF MY PARENTS.
SOMETIMES, IT TAKES THE REALLY BAD TIMES TO MAKE YOU APPRECIATE THE GOOD ONES.

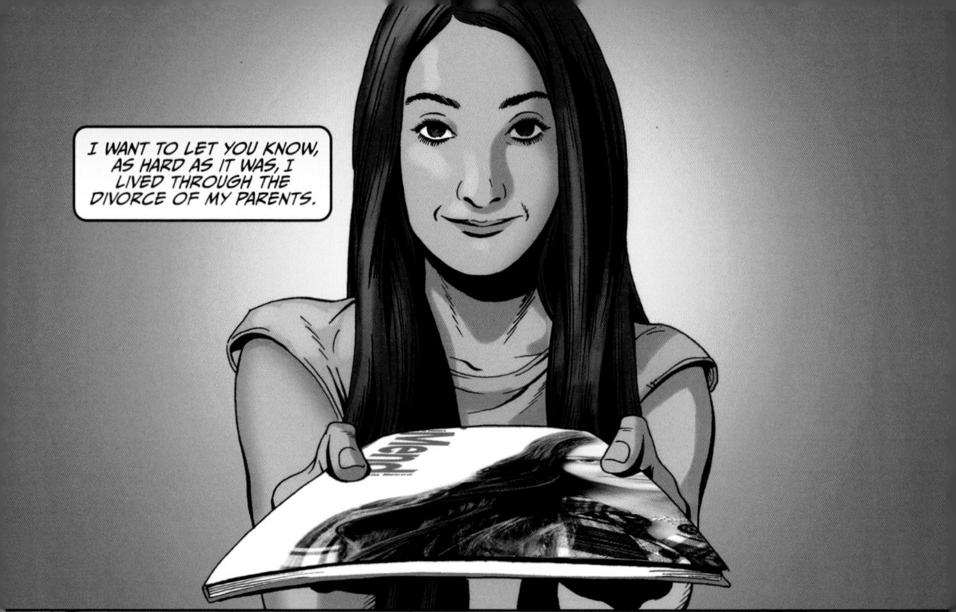
I WANT TO LET YOU KNOW, AS HARD AS IT WAS, I LIVED THROUGH THE DIVORCE OF MY PARENTS.

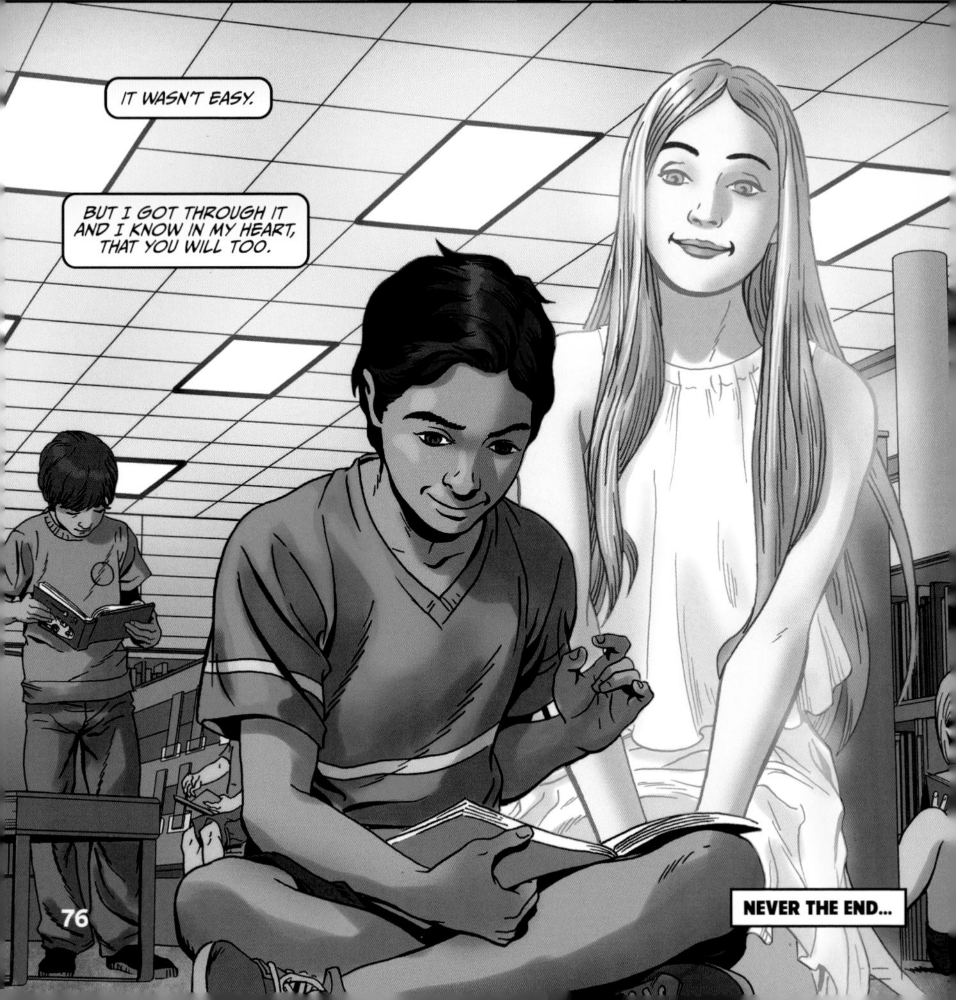
IT WASN'T EASY.
BUT I GOT THROUGH IT AND I KNOW IN MY HEART, THAT YOU WILL TOO.
NEVER THE END...

ABOUT OUR AUTHOR

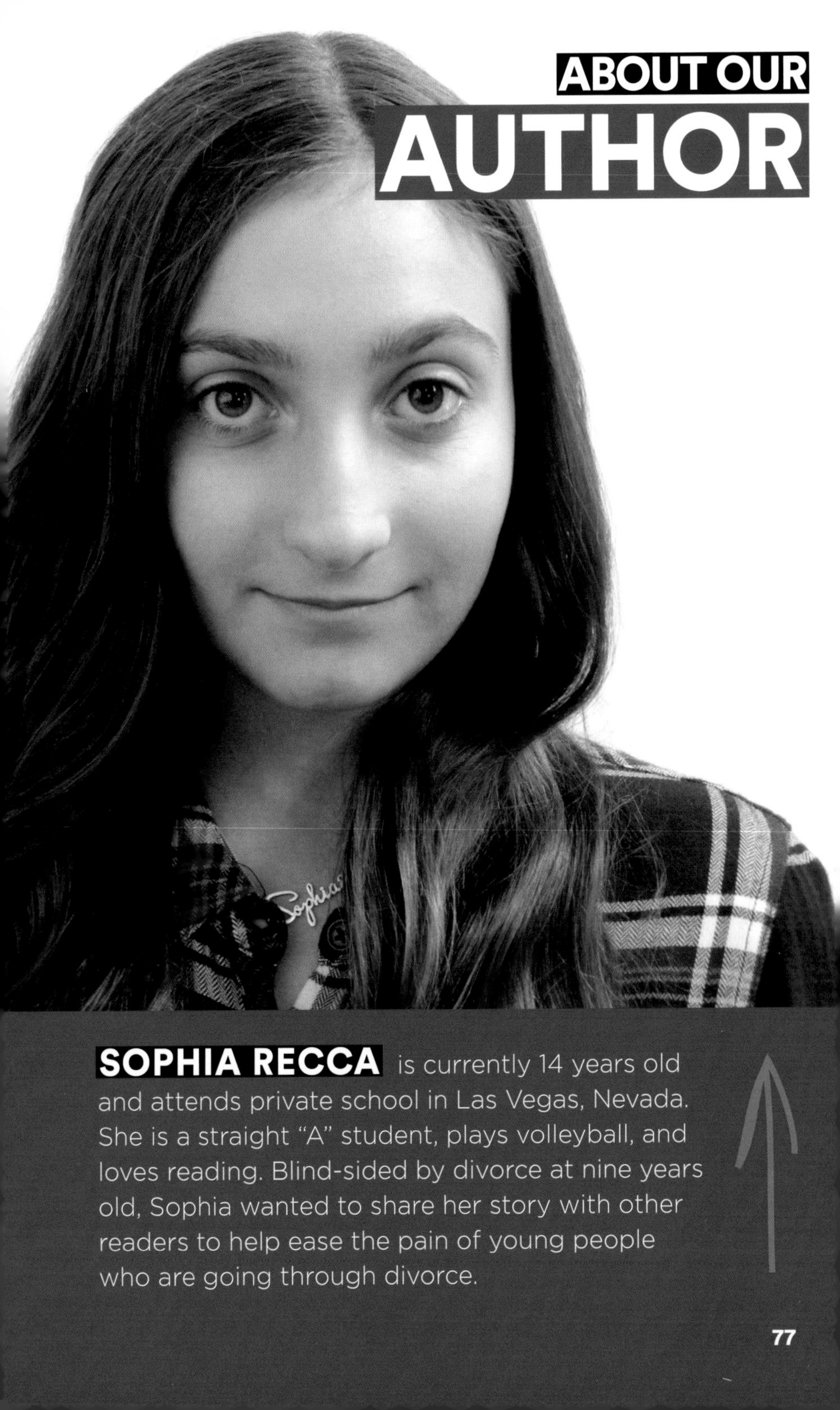
Sophia

SOPHIA RECCA is currently 14 years old and attends private school in Las Vegas, Nevada. She is a straight "A" student, plays volleyball, and loves reading. Blind-sided by divorce at nine years old, Sophia wanted to share her story with other readers to help ease the pain of young people who are going through divorce.

SOPHIA...

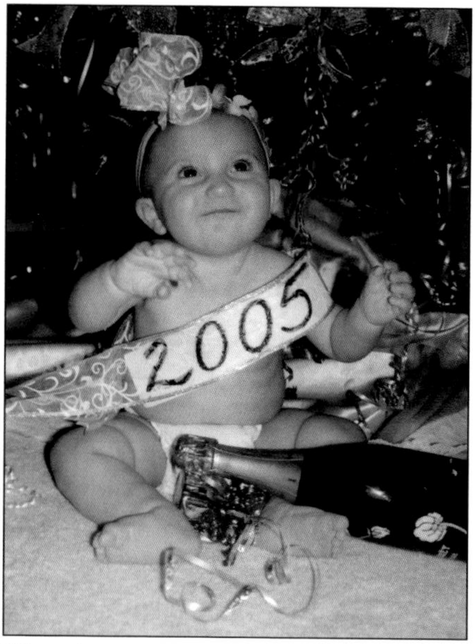
2005

When I was one I had no hair, so I wore headbands in photos.

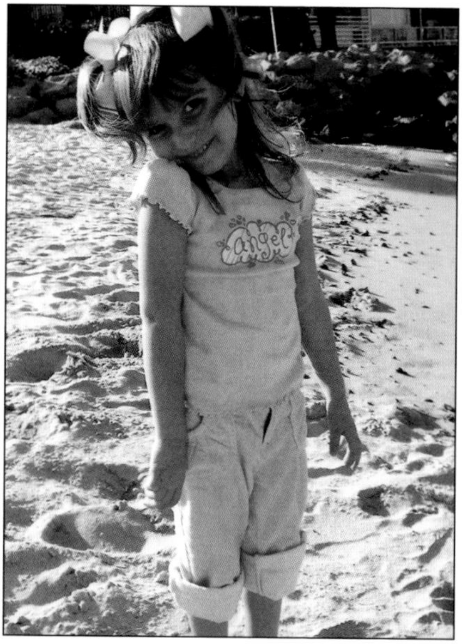
Angel

I love taking pictures on the beach because I get to send them to my dad!

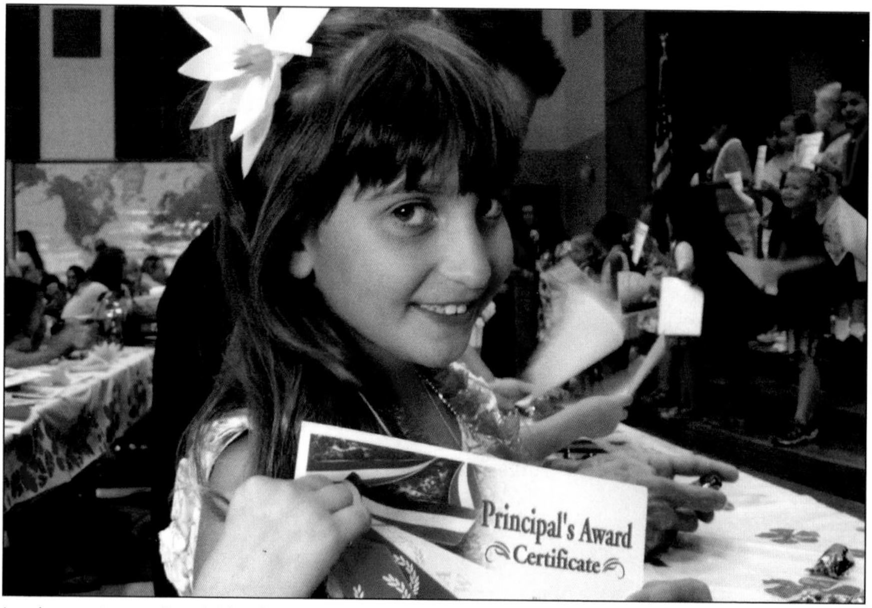
Principal's Award
Certificate

In elementary school, I had amazing grades and won an award from the principal!

...SOPHIA

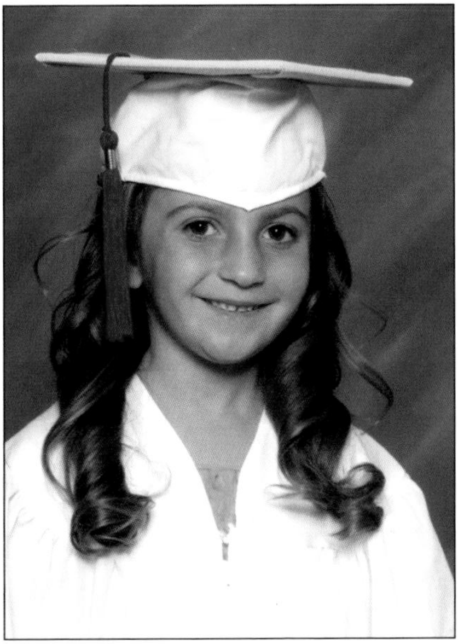

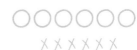

Preschool was so much fun, but sadly, I had to move on to kindergarten.

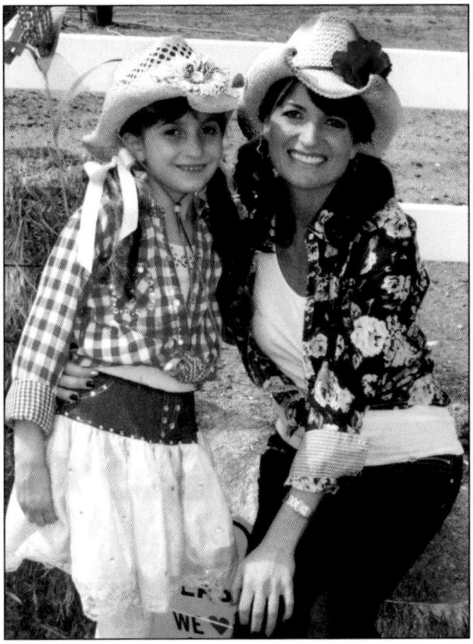

One year, for my birthday, I got to be a cowgirl and ride real horses!

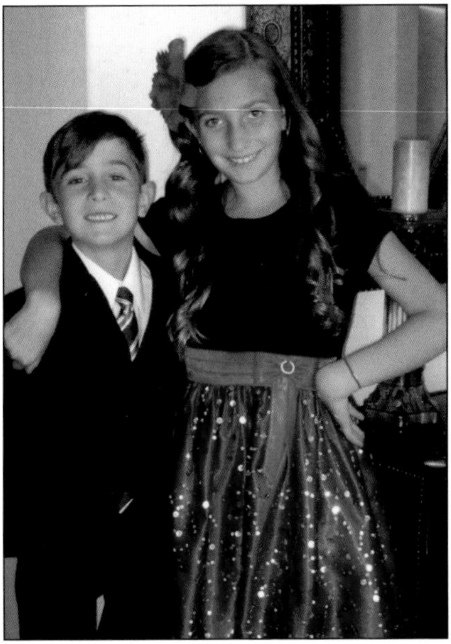

I've already had my First Communion but now it's my brother's turn!

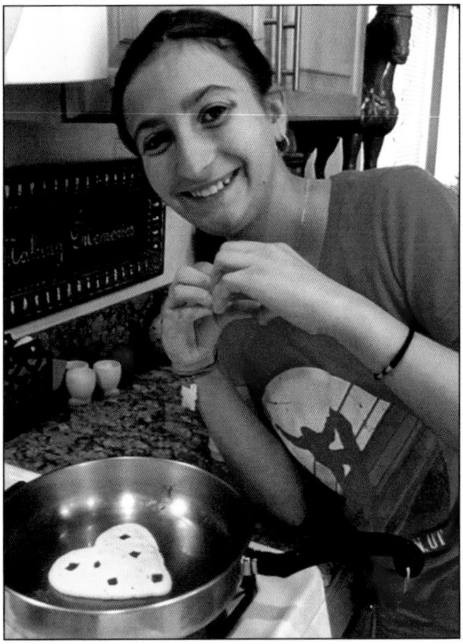

I'm a great cook, so I used my amazing skills for my mother on Mother's Day.

SOPHIA...

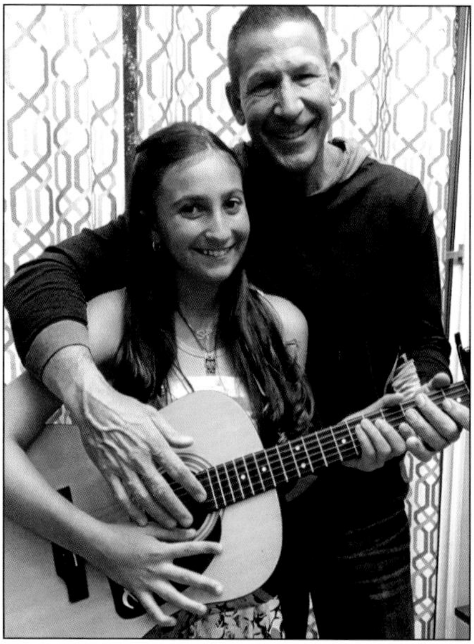

My dad loves when I play the guitar, even if I'm still learning!

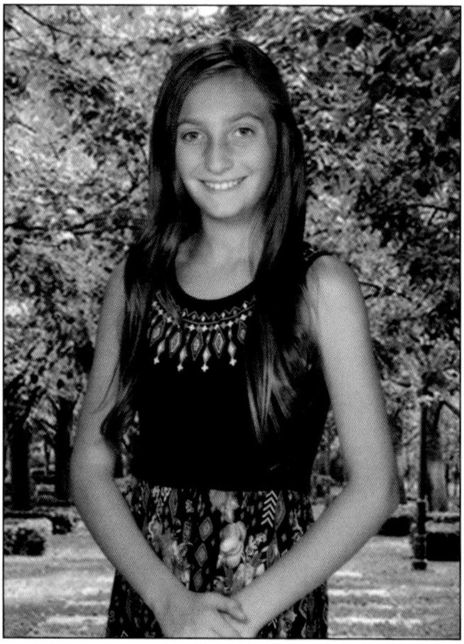

School picture day is so much fun because I get to see all of my friends dressed up!

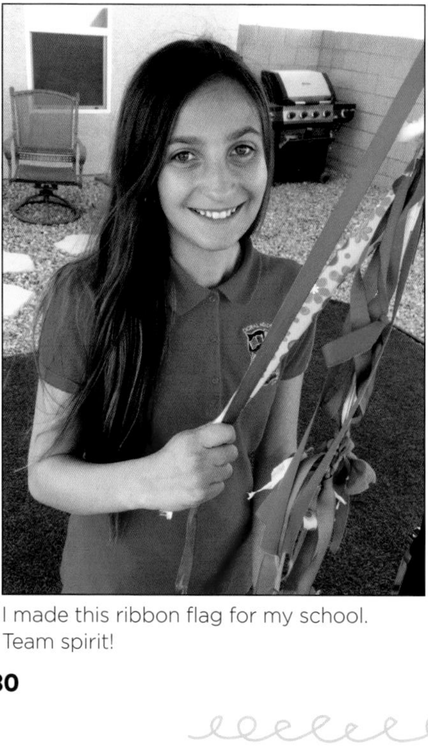

I made this ribbon flag for my school. Team spirit!

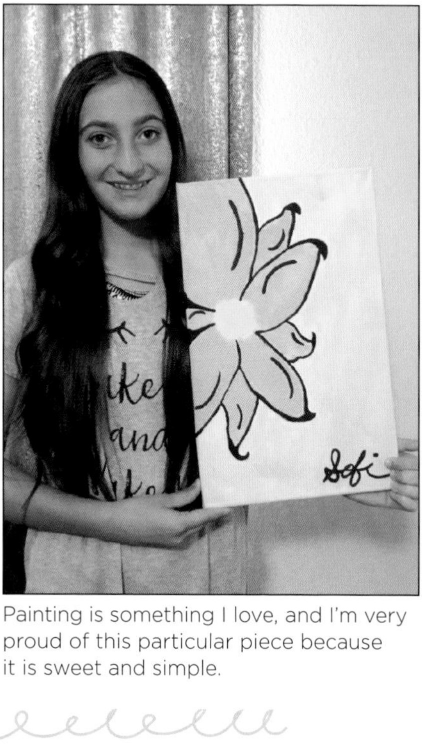
Sofi

Painting is something I love, and I'm very proud of this particular piece because it is sweet and simple.

TAKE 5!

FIVE PARENT TAKE-AWAYS ABOUT DIVORCE

DENIS SCINTA

is a family lawyer who's been practicing law for over 35 years in the Greater Amherst area of Buffalo, New York.

YOUR CHILD NEEDS "BOTH" PARENTS. NOT THE MOST LIKED IN THE MOMENT.

The knee-jerk reaction for adults with kids who get divorced is to wage war through the kids. This is a huge mistake. The best thing to do early in the divorce is to reassure your child that both parents will continue to be in their lives, settle on a custody schedule, and honor it with consistency.

DEEP DOWN, THE CHILD WILL THINK IT'S THEIR FAULT. REMEMBER THAT.

Children don't have the emotional maturity to process their parents divorcing. Most kids believe "it's because of me." Constant reassurance that the split has nothing to do with the child cannot be overstated. The sooner you alleviate this from the child's heart and mind, the better.

ACT LIKE THE ADULT, NOT THE CHILD. THEY NEED PARENTS NOW MORE THAN EVER.

Divorce usually brings out the worst in the adult. The stress of financial and emotional warfare will keep the parents in constant "battle mode." Whatever you do, do not wage war by using your children as a "messenger" to hurt the other parent. Keep the kids out of the middle.

"CO-PARENTING" IS FOR THE BENEFIT OF THE CHILD, NOT YOU. ACT AS IF...

Parenting together will establish consistency and peace between both households. It's important for parents to support each other in front of the children. Learn to say "Yes" more than "No" and put your child's needs first. Co-parenting will set the child's mind at ease that they still have both parents in their lives for the long haul.

THE DAMAGE YOU DO TO THEM WILL LAST A LIFETIME. LEARN TO COUNT TO 10.

Keep the mudslinging and parent critiquing at zero. If you find yourself hearing something from your child that "came from Mom" or "from Dad," bite your tongue and count to ten. Children, sometimes, find themselves reporting or relaying messages from the other household. Although you may be fuming inside, you'll just have to learn to "table it" until you can speak to the other parent directly. And never in the presence of the child...

THE STORY DOESN'T END HERE...

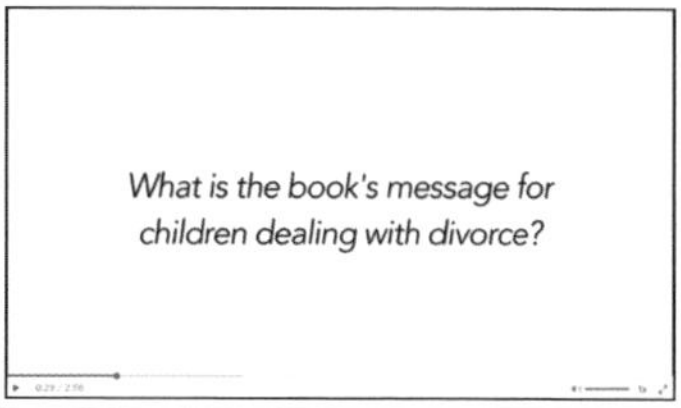

What is the book's message for children dealing with divorce?

VISIT
ZUIKERPRESS.COM

To learn more about Sophia's story, see behind-the-scenes videos of Sophia and her family and learn more about how to cope with **DIVORCE** in your family.

Our **WEBSITE** is another resource to help our readers deal with the issues that they face every day. Log on to find advice from experts, links to helpful organizations and literature, and more real-life experiences from young people just like you.

Spotlighting young writers with heartfelt stories that enlighten and inspire.

Los Angeles

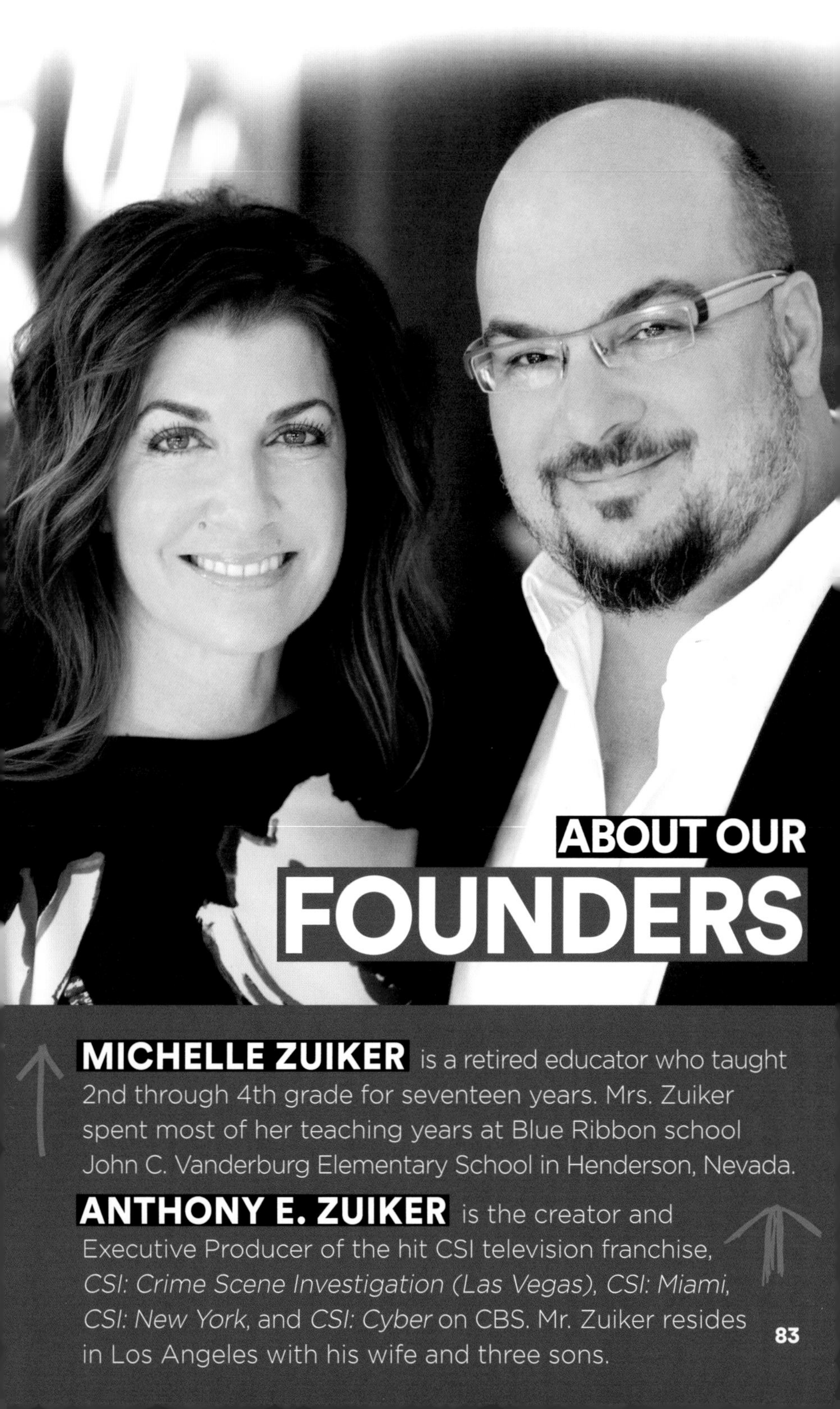

ABOUT OUR FOUNDERS

MICHELLE ZUIKER is a retired educator who taught 2nd through 4th grade for seventeen years. Mrs. Zuiker spent most of her teaching years at Blue Ribbon school John C. Vanderburg Elementary School in Henderson, Nevada.

ANTHONY E. ZUIKER is the creator and Executive Producer of the hit CSI television franchise, *CSI: Crime Scene Investigation (Las Vegas)*, *CSI: Miami*, *CSI: New York*, and *CSI: Cyber* on CBS. Mr. Zuiker resides in Los Angeles with his wife and three sons.

ABOUT OUR
ILLUSTRATORS
& EDITOR...

NAM KIM-PENCILER

is a Philadelphia-based artist, founder and director of Studio Imaginary Lines, an all-purpose design house which produces original content for comic books, video games, mobile apps and commercial advertising. Nam is a self-taught illustrator who credits artists such as Burne Hogarth, Jim Lee and Masamune Shiro for shaping his artistic style and vision. He has worked for Nike, ToykoPop, Radical Publishing and Image Comics where he illustrated the critically acclaimed *Samurai's Blood*.

GARRY LEACH-INKER

is a British artist best known for his work co-creating the new *Marvelman* with writer Alan Moore. As an artist Garry was a frequent contributor to *2000AD* working on *Dan Dare*, *Judge Dredd*, *The V.C.s* and *Future Shocks*. At DC Comics Garry worked on *Legion of Superheroes*, *Hit Man*, *Monarchy* and *Global Frequency,* while over at Marvel Comics, he inked Chris Weston on *The Twelve*. Garry has been a cover artist for Marvel, DC, *2000AD*, *Eclipse*, *Dynamic Forces*, and Kellogg's Corn Flakes.

FAHRIZA KAMAPUTRA– COLORIST

was born and raised in southern Jakarta. In 2010 he worked as colorist on a local comic book *Vienetta and the Stupid Aliens* which led to his work on the web comic *Rokki* and Madeleine Holly-Rosling's *Boston Metaphysical Society* with the studio STELLAR LABS. Fahriza now works as a freelance artist.

DAVE ELLIOTT–EDITOR

has worked on such diverse titles as *A1, Deadline, Viz, Heavy Metal, 2000AD, Justice League of America, Transformers, GI Joe, The Real Ghostbusters* and *Doctor Who*. Dave co-founded Radical Studios where he oversaw the development and launch of Radical's premiere comic book titles several of which were sold as film properties including *Hercules, Freedom Formula* and *Oblivion*. He recently launched the graphic novel series *Odyssey* and *The Weirding Willows* with Titan Comics.

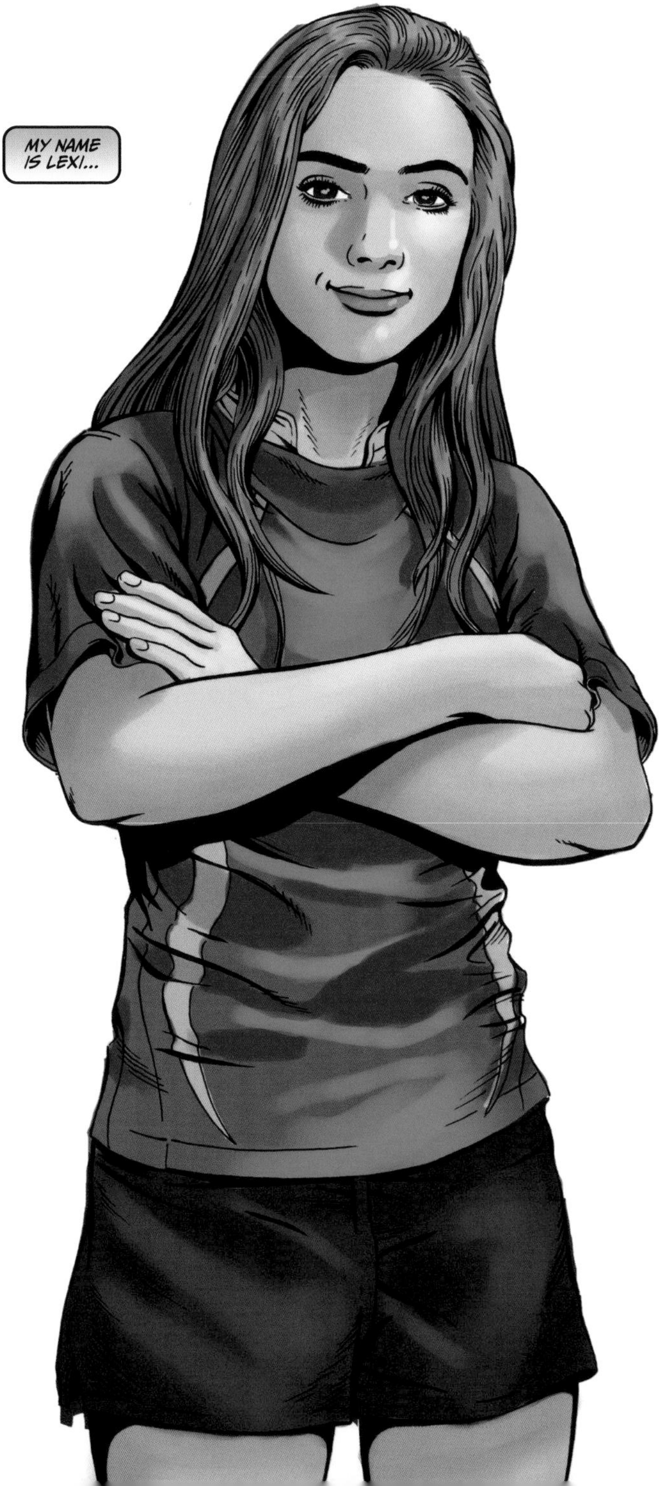
MY NAME IS LEXI...

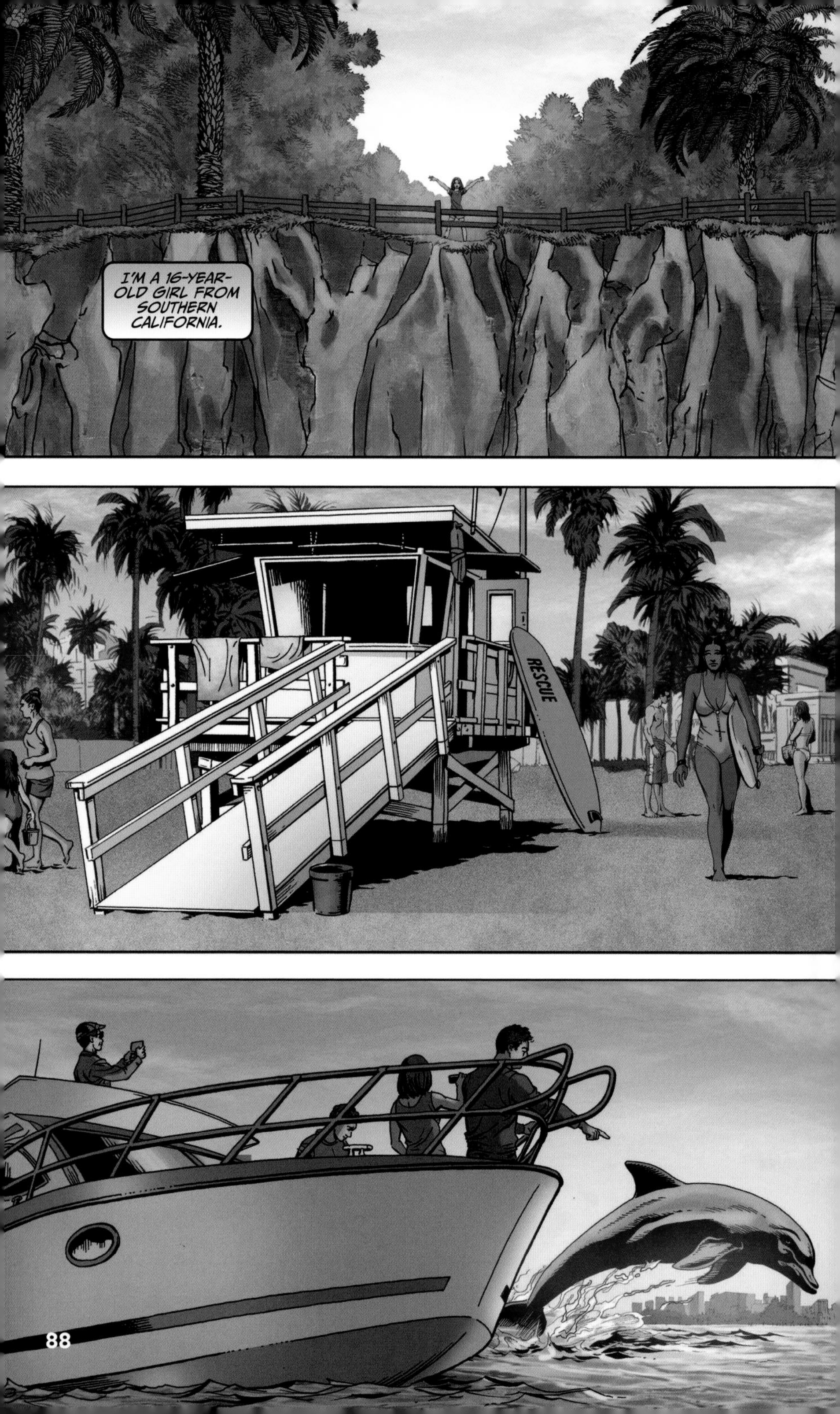
I'M A 16-YEAR-OLD GIRL FROM SOUTHERN CALIFORNIA.
RESCUE

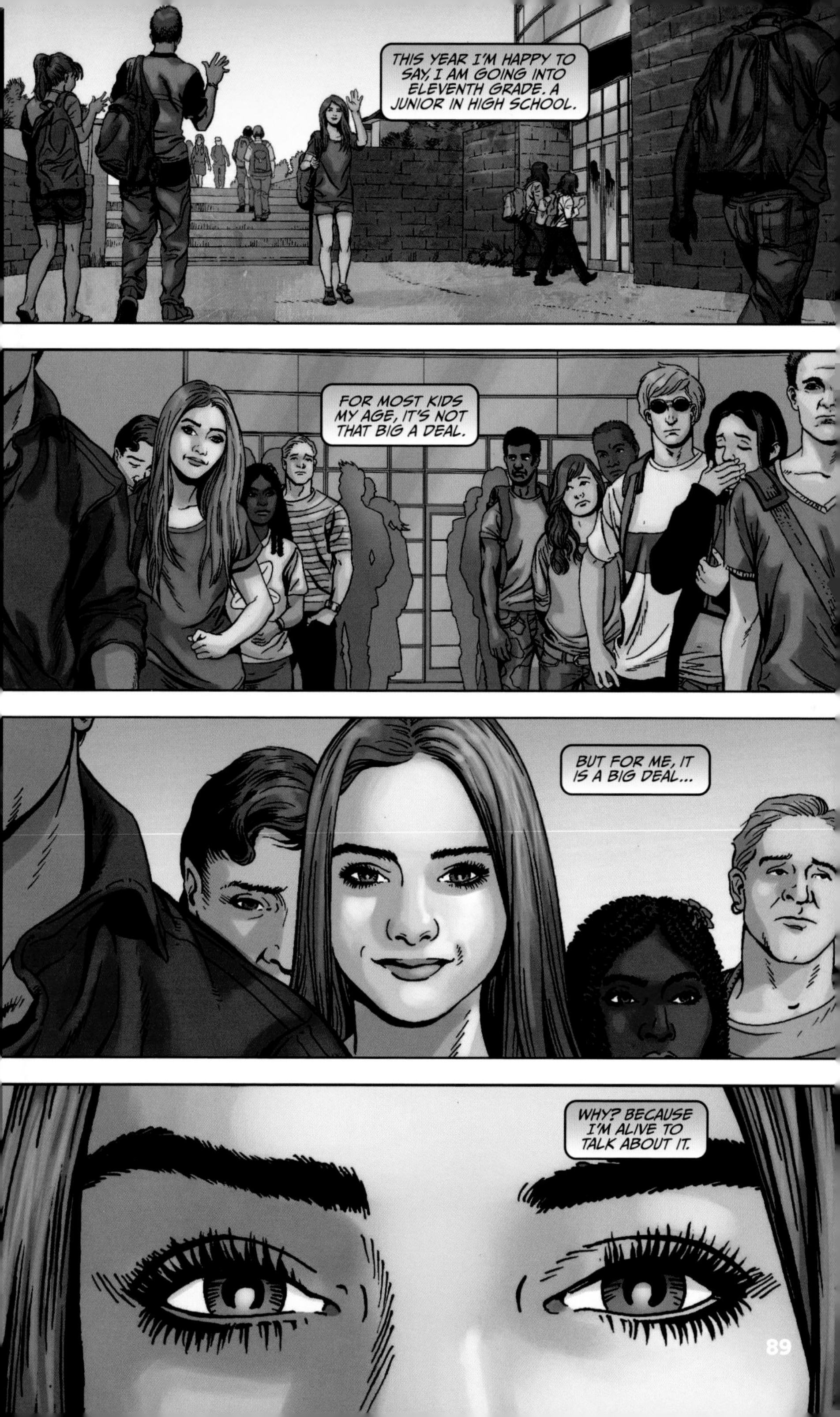
THIS YEAR I'M HAPPY TO SAY, I AM GOING INTO ELEVENTH GRADE. A JUNIOR IN HIGH SCHOOL.
FOR MOST KIDS MY AGE, IT'S NOT THAT BIG A DEAL.
BUT FOR ME, IT IS A BIG DEAL...
WHY? BECAUSE I'M ALIVE TO TALK ABOUT IT.

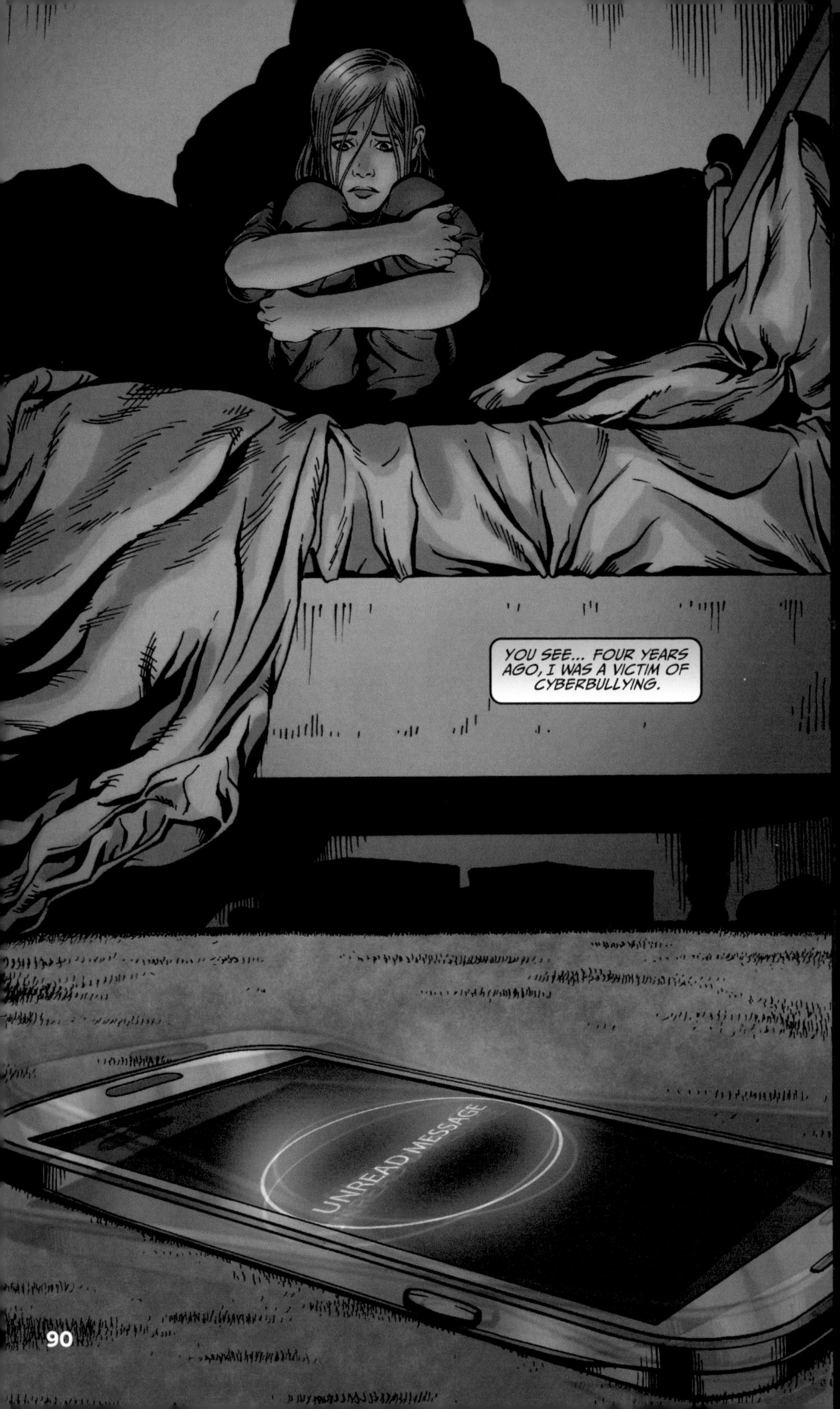
YOU SEE... FOUR YEARS AGO, I WAS A VICTIM OF CYBERBULLYING.
UNREAD MESSAGE

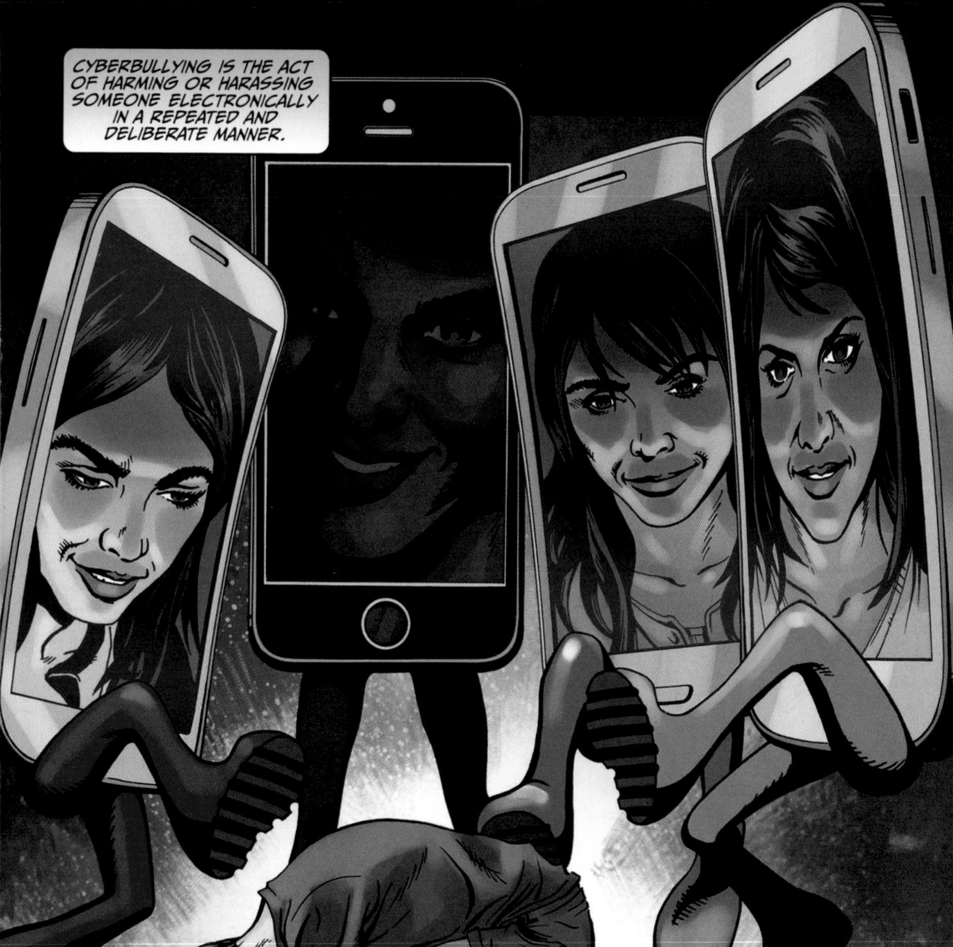
CYBERBULLYING IS THE ACT OF HARMING OR HARASSING SOMEONE ELECTRONICALLY IN A REPEATED AND DELIBERATE MANNER.
I WAS HARASSED, HUMILIATED, AND MENTALLY ABUSED BY A GROUP OF GIRLS WHO I REALLY THOUGHT WERE MY FRIENDS.

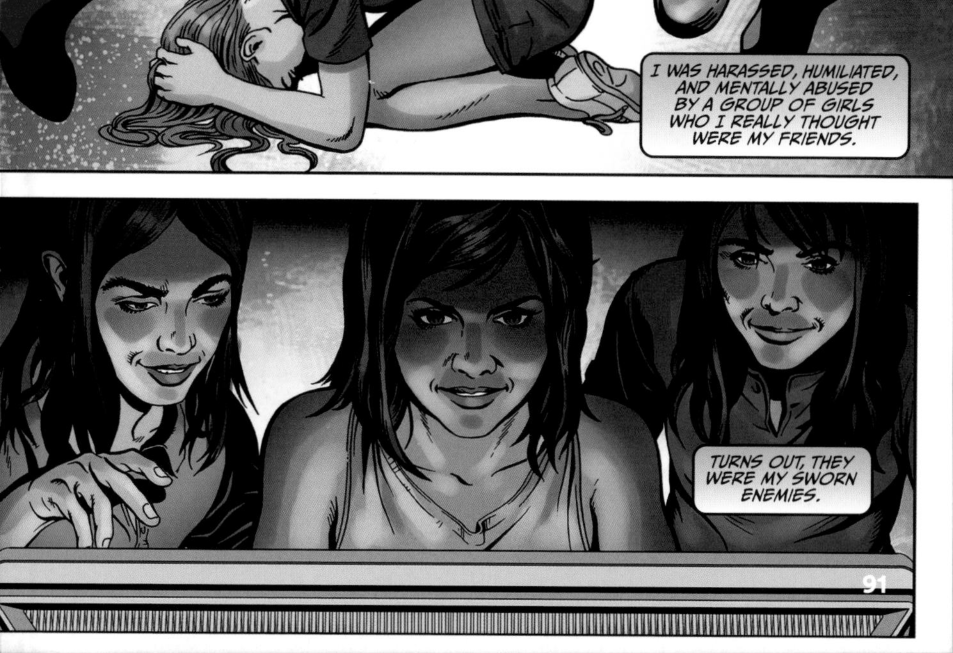
TURNS OUT, THEY WERE MY SWORN ENEMIES.

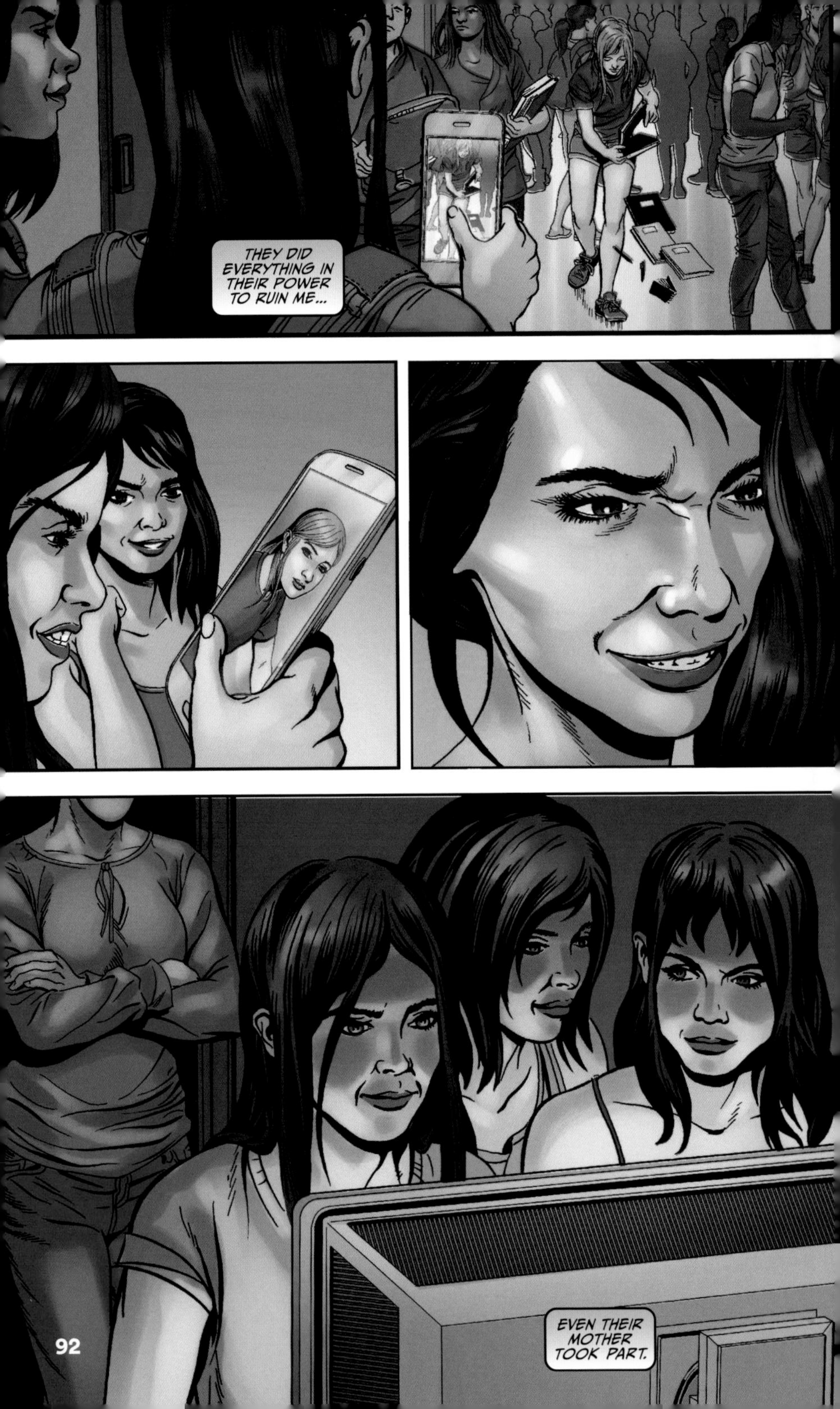
THEY DID EVERYTHING IN THEIR POWER TO RUIN ME...
EVEN THEIR MOTHER TOOK PART.

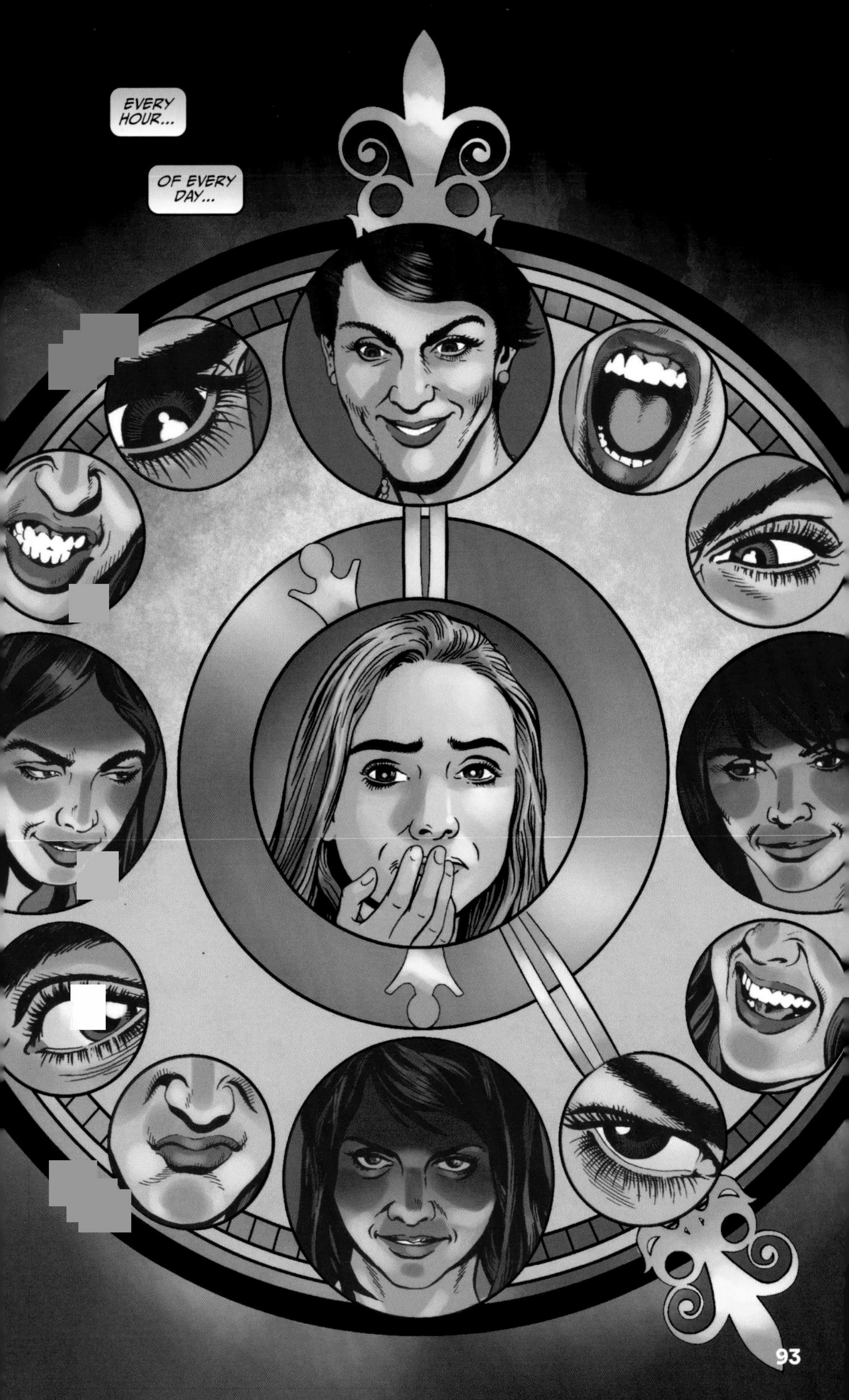
EVERY HOUR...
OF EVERY DAY...

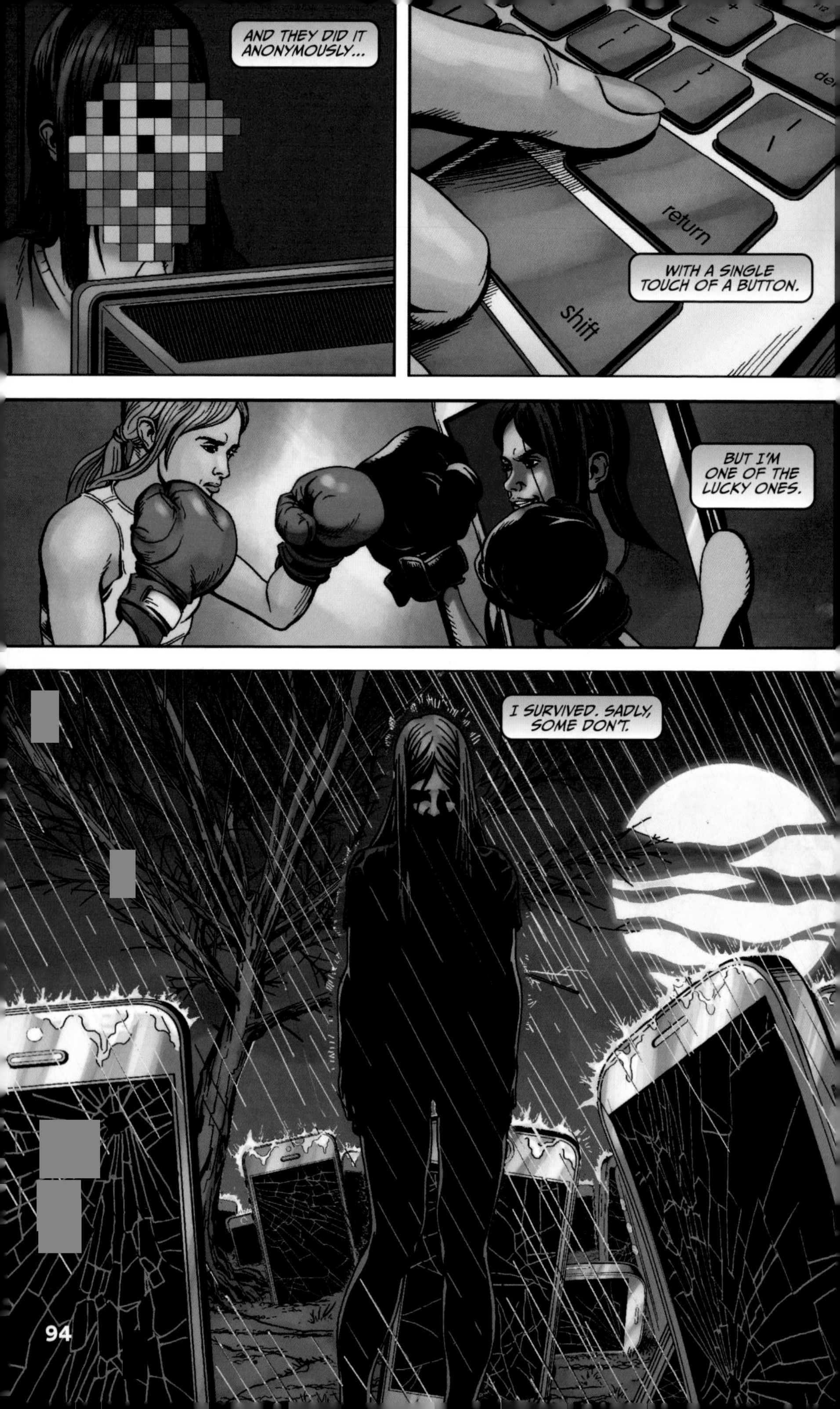
AND THEY DID IT ANONYMOUSLY...
return
shift
WITH A SINGLE TOUCH OF A BUTTON.
BUT I'M ONE OF THE LUCKY ONES.
I SURVIVED. SADLY, SOME DON'T.

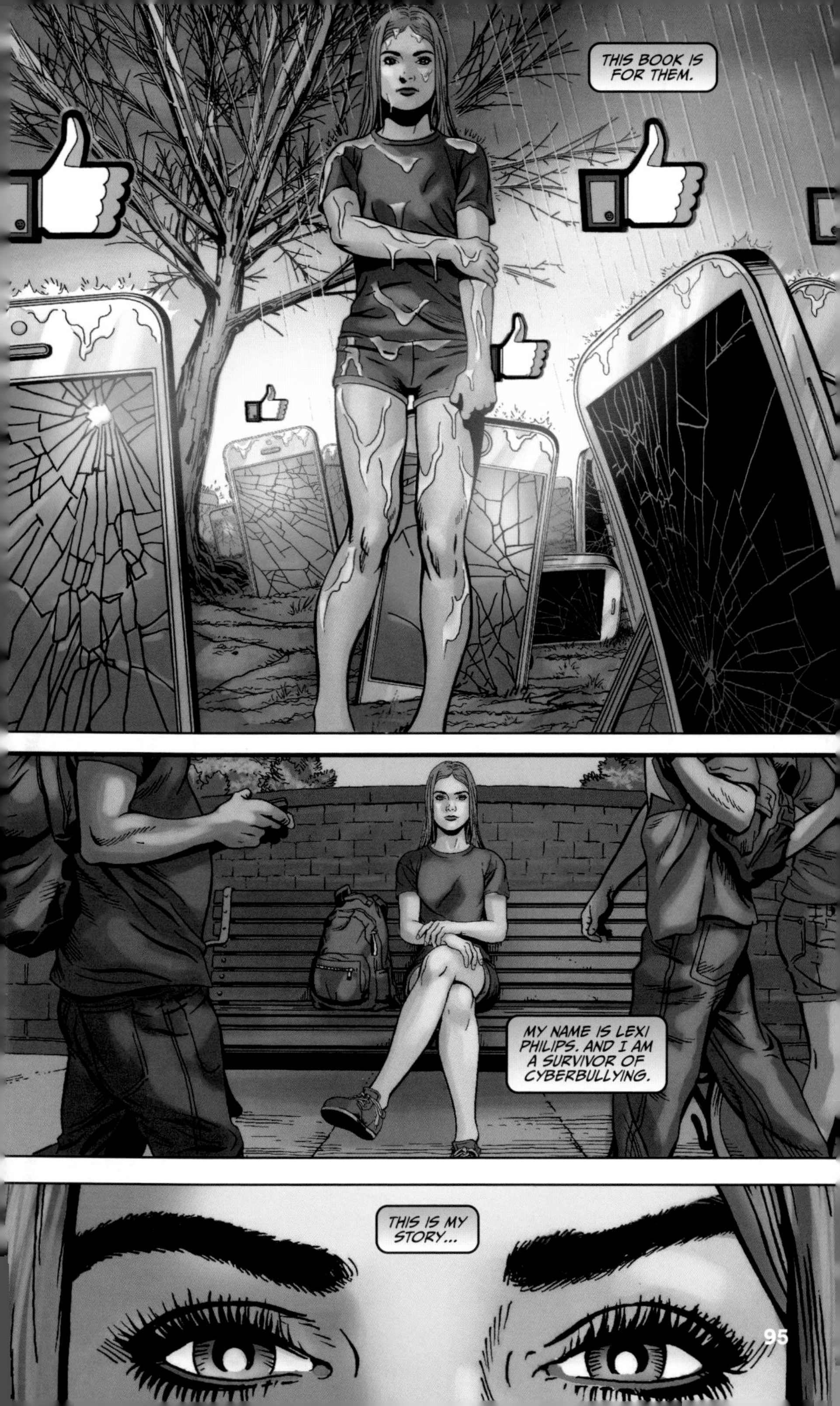
THIS BOOK IS FOR THEM.
MY NAME IS LEXI PHILIPS. AND I AM A SURVIVOR OF CYBERBULLYING.
THIS IS MY STORY...

NEW FOR FALL 2018

MEND: A STORY OF DIVORCE

CLICK: A STORY OF CYBERBULLYING

COMING SPRING 2019

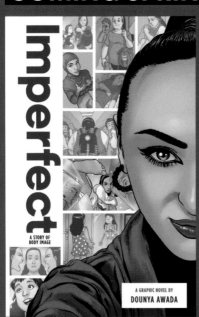

IMPERFECT: A STORY OF BODY IMAGE

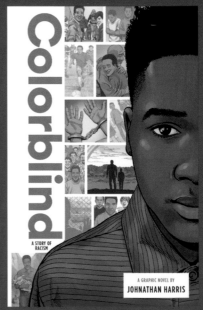

COLORBLIND: A STORY OF RACISM